HARDPRESS.NET
HOME OF HARD-TO-FIND BOOKS

The Law Relating to Benefit Building Societies
by William Tidd Pratt

Address:
HardPress
8345 NW 66TH ST #2561
MIAMI FL 33166-2626
USA
Email: info@hardpress.net

THE LAW

OF

BENEFIT BUILDING

SOCIETIES

W. TIDD PRATT

BENEFIT BUILDING SOCIETIES.

LONDON
PRINTED BY SPOTTISWOODE AND CO.
NEW-STREET SQUARE

THE LAW

RELATING TO

BENEFIT BUILDING SOCIETIES

(6 & 7 WILL. IV. c. 32)

WITH PRACTICAL OBSERVATIONS ON THE ACT AND
ALL THE CASES DECIDED THEREON:

TOGETHER WITH

A FORM OF RULES FOR A PERMANENT BENEFIT BUILDING SOCIETY

AND

FORMS OF MORTGAGES TO THE TRUSTEES.

By W. TIDD PRATT, Esq.

OF THE INNER TEMPLE, BARRISTER-AT-LAW.

SECOND EDITION.

LONDON:
LONGMAN, GREEN, LONGMAN, ROBERTS & GREEN.
1865.

TO

THE REGISTRAR OF FRIENDLY SOCIETIES

IN ENGLAND

THE FOLLOWING WORK IS DEDICATED

BY HIS SON

THE AUTHOR.

CONTENTS.

———◆———

•

TABLE OF CASES.

BENEFIT BUILDING SOCIETIES.

PART I.

NATURE AND FORMATION OF BENEFIT BUILDING SOCIETIES.

A Benefit Building Society is in the nature of a Joint Stock Association, the members of which subscribe periodically, and in proportion to the number of their shares, different sums into one common fund, which thus becomes large enough to be advantageously employed, by being lent out at interest to such of the members as desire advances; and the interest as soon as it is received, making fresh capital, is lent out again and again so as to be continually reproductive. The payments of borrowing members should be so calculated as to enable them to repay, by equal monthly instalments within a specified period, the principal of the sums borrowed with interest. The other members who have not received advances, become entitled, at the end of a given number of years, to be paid a sum equivalent to the amount of their payments, with accumulated compound interest.

The Act regulating these societies is the 6 & 7 *W.* 4. c. 32, by which it is enacted that any number

B

of persons may form a society for the purpose of raising, by monthly or other subscriptions of the several members, shares not exceeding the value of 150*l.* for each share, such subscriptions not to exceed in the whole 20*s.* per month for each share, a stock or fund for the purpose of enabling each member to receive out of the funds the amount or value of his or her share or shares therein, to erect or purchase one or more dwelling-house or houses, or other real or leasehold estate, to be secured by way of mortgage to the society until the amount or value of his or her shares shall have been fully repaid to the society, with the interest thereon, and all fines or other payments incurred in respect thereof.

The society is empowered to make rules, which must be duly certified by the Registrar of Friendly Societies ; and for this purpose two copies of the rules, signed by three members and the secretary, must be sent to him, and if he finds them conformable to law he is to give his certificate on each of the copies, and to return one to the society and send the other to the Clerk of the Peace for the county wherein the society is established. The same course is to be adopted upon the making of any alterations or amendments in the rules ; and an affidavit of the clerk or secretary or one of the officers of the society that the provisions of the Act have been complied with must also be sent.

The special advantages guaranteed to societies established under this Act are as follows :—

1. The rules are binding upon the members, and may be legally enforced.

2. Protection is given to the members in enforcing their just claims, and against any fraudulent dissolution of the society.

3. The property of the society is declared to be vested in the trustees or treasurer for the time being.

4. The trustees or treasurer may, with respect to the property of the society, sue and be sued in their or his own names or name.

5. Fraud committed with respect to the property of the society is punishable by justices.

6. Disputes in certain cases are to be settled by reference to justices or arbitrators, whose order or award is final.

7. Priority of payment of debts, in case of the death or bankruptcy of any officer of the society, or upon an execution being issued against his property.

8. Any sum not exceeding 20*l.* may, upon the death of a member, be paid without letters of administration.

9. Members are allowed to be witnesses in all proceedings, criminal or civil, respecting the property of the society.

10. Exemption from stamp duty of all securities given to the society.

And lastly, no reconveyance of the mortgaged property is necessary on the termination of the society, or the repayment of the money advanced.

The rules are required by the Act to contain the following particulars, namely, the intents and purposes of the society ; to what uses the funds are to be appropriated, and the imposition of a penalty

upon their misappropriation; the place or places of
the meetings of the society; the powers and duties
of the members at large, and of the committees and
officers; the number of officers, and the purposes for
and the manner in which they are to be elected, and
their duration in office, as also the number of members to constitute the committee; the manner of
settling disputes, whether by justices or arbitration,
and if in the latter way the number of arbitrators
and the mode of their election.   Provision must also
be made for the preparation, by some officer of the
society, once in every year, of a statement of the
funds and effects of the society, specifying in whose
custody they are, together with an account of all
receipts and expenses since the last preceding statement.

The provisions of the former Friendly Societies
Acts, the 10 *Geo.* 4. c. 56, and 4 & 5 *Wm.* 4. c. 40,
are incorporated into the Benefit Building Societies
Act; and, although these Acts have been repealed,
they are still in force for the purposes of these
societies.   This point was virtually decided in *Rex*
v. *Inhabitants of Merionethshire,* 6 Q.B. Reports 343,
where it was held that the repeal of an Act which
had been incorporated with another Act did not
repeal the former Act so far as it was applicable to
the purposes of the Act into which it had been
incorporated.   See also *Reg.* v. *Stock,* 8 Ad. & Ell.
405.

The sections of the above Acts applicable to these
societies will be found *infra.*

By the 7th section of the 10 *Geo.* 4. c. 56, no

society is to have the benefit of the Act until the rules have been deposited with the Clerk of the Peace, and duly entered in a book to be kept by an officer of the society ; but notwithstanding this, any bond or security given to the treasurer will be valid, and may be sued upon at law. This point arose in the case of *Jones* v. *Woollam*, 5 Barn. & Ald. 769, where it was held that a bond given to the treasurer of a Benefit Society, for the use of the society, was an available security at common law, although the rules of the society had not been confirmed pursuant to the statute then in force relating to Friendly Societies. In *Margett* v. *Parkes*, 1 Dowl. & L. 582, which was an action of assumpsit by the treasurer of a Friendly Society on a note, it was held that an averment that the rules were filed under 10 *Geo.* 4. c. 56, before the making of the promise, was not material ; and an objection that they were not filed until after the making of the note, but before it became due, was invalid.

It would seem, upon the principle of the following case, that if any security requiring a stamp is given to the society before the rules are certified, and is not properly stamped, it will be sufficient if they are duly certified before action brought. In *Bradburne* v. *Whitbread*, 6 Sc. N. R. p. 284, which was the case of an unstamped promissory note given to the trustees of a Loan Society established under the Friendly Loan Act, it was contended that the trustees could not sue on the note, it having been made before the rules were enrolled, though after they had been certified ; but the Court held that the enrolment of the rules before the commencement of the action, was sufficient to enable the trustees to recover.

Until the rules and alterations of rules are certified, they cannot be legally acted on. This point arose in *Battey* v. *Townrow*, 4 Camp. 5, where it was held that an action could not be maintained by the trustees of a Friendly Society, elected under new regulations, until they had been confirmed according to the statute, as the plaintiffs were not the legal trustees of the society for the time being, and the effects sought to be recovered never vested in them. See also *Wybergh* v. *Ainley*, 4 M'Cleland, 699. In *Reg.* v. *Godolphin*, 8 Ad. & Ell. 338, it appeared that certain alterations were made in the rules of a Friendly Society established under the 33 *Geo.* 3. c. 54; but the altered rules were never enrolled, and it was held that the rules as altered could not legally be acted upon. In giving judgment, the Court said it would be well if it were generally understood that these societies cannot depart from their established rules, or neglect to comply with the statute in the mode of altering or repealing them, without exposing their property to damage, and themselves to great expense, loss, and inconvenience. A doubt was also entertained as to whether the original rules continued in force, even for the purpose of holding the society legal under the statute, in consequence of the case *Ex parte Norrish*, Jac. 162; but in the case of *Reg.* v. *Cotton*, 15 Q.B. Repts. 569, it was held that, notwithstanding the alterations, the society was still in existence.

See also *Meredith* v. *Whittingham,* 1 Com. Bench Reports, N. S. 216.

All rules and alterations are binding from the time of their being certified, *Bradburne* v. *Whitbread,* 6 Scott, N.C. 283, and the certificate of the barrister is conclusive as to the validity of the rules or alterations, *Dewhurst* v. *Clarkson,* 3 Ell. & Bl. 194, where it was proved that the rule of the society as to manner of making new rules had not been complied with; the certificate, however, will not make an illegal rule legal, *Kelsall* v. *Tyler,* 11 Exc. Rep. 560.

The property on account of which the advance is required, is to be mortgaged to the society to secure the amount of the shares with interest, and all other payments due under the rules; the security should be made in the usual mortgage form, and not as a conveyance upon trusts to secure the repayments, for if made in this latter form the society will not, upon default being made in the repayments, be entitled to a foreclosure decree, as in the case of a regular mortgage, but accounts will be ordered to be taken and the property to be sold, *Schwestzen* v. *Stych,* 31 Beav. 37.

The funds of the society cannot be laid out in the purchase of land to be allotted among the members, and the directors and trustees will be personally liable for all monies so laid out, *Grimes* v. *Harrison,* 26 Beav. 435, *In re Kent Benefit Building Society,* 7 Jur. 1045; but notwithstanding this misapplication of the funds, the members are still liable to pay their subscriptions, *Hughes* v. *Layton,* 10 Jur. 513, 12 Weekly Rep. 408.

By the 5th section of the Building Societies Act, a receipt endorsed upon the mortgage or further charge is to vacate the same, and to vest the property in the person for the time being entitled to the equity of redemption. In *Prosser v. Rice*, 28 Beav. 68, a member mortgaged to the society and then made a second mortgage to C, who therefore became entitled to the equity of redemption; the member then borrowed a sum from D to pay off the society, and a receipt was endorsed upon the mortgage, and a mortgage executed to D; and it was held that the legal estate was thereupon vested in C by the operation of this section, and not in D. Although this receipt operates as an effectual reconveyance, yet in a recent case the costs of a reconveyance by deed were allowed on taxation. *Page, In re*, 32 Beav. 485.

These societies are within the operation of the Winding-up Clause of the Joint Stock Companies Act, 1862. *In re Midland Counties Benefit Building Society*, 33 Law Jour. (Ch.) 739.

PART II.

RIGHTS AND LIABILITIES OF THE SOCIETY AND ITS OFFICERS.

The 13th section of the 10 *Geo.* 4. c. 56, states how the funds of the society not wanted for the immediate exigencies thereof may be invested, and upon the construction of this section it has been held that the society may lend such funds upon mortgage to any of its members, and that such security will vest in the trustees for the time being, *Morrison* v. *Glover*, 4 Exc. Rep. 431, 19 Law Jour. (Exc.) 20; *Cutbill* v. *Kingdom*, 1 Exc. Rep. 494.

By the 11th section the treasurer is to give security to the society for the due performance of his duties, but this will not make him liable for monies received on account of the society, and of which he may have been robbed by violence and without fault of his own, the obligation imposed by this section being that only of a bailee, *Walker* v. *Guarantee Society*, 18 Q.B. Rep. 277.

The 21st section of the above Act, vesting all the property in the trustees of the society, has been held to empower them to call for a transfer of the funds belonging to the society previously to its legal establishment, if a majority of the members agree to the society being brought under the Act, *Yeates* v. *Roberts*, 3 Dre. 171, 7 De Gex, M. & G. 227; *Hodges* v. *Wale*, 2 Weekly Rep. 65. The property, however, of a society in the hands of other persons does not vest in the trustees by their mere appointment, *Dewhurst* v. *Clarkson*, 3 Ell. & Bl. 194.

This section makes the continuing and new trustees joint tenants, and operates as a new appointment of all, *Walker* v. *Giles*, 6 C. B. Rep. 662; and no assignment or conveyance is necessary upon the appointment of new trustees, *Morrison* v. *Glover*, 16 L. J. (Exc.) 20; *Reg.* v. *Cain*, 1 Car. & M. 309. By this section no action can be brought or defended by the trustees without the consent of a meeting; but in *Doe* v. *Glover*, 15 Q.B. Rep. 103, it was held that the defendant, a member, could not allege that the action was brought without such consent. Upon an action on a note made payable to the treasurer for the time being, it was held that it should have been brought by the treasurer at the time of the action, *Timms* v. *Williams*, 3 Q.B. Rep. 413. It was held in a late case, *Hodges* v. *Wale*, 2 Weekly Rep. 65, that a power by the rules to appoint trustees from time to time implied a power of removal.

In proceedings before justices under section 25, the complaint must be made and information laid within six calendar months from the time when the matter of such complaint arose, 11 & 12 *Vic.* c. 43, s. 11; 12 & 13 *Vic.* c. 70, s. 11; and by 2 & 3 *Vic.* c. 71, s. 14, and 11 & 12 *Vic.* c. 43, s. 34; the Lord Mayor of London and any Alderman sitting at the Mansion House or at Guildhall, may do alone any act which under this section may be done by more than one justice; and by 11 & 12 *Vic.* c. 43, s. 33, any one Metropolitan Police magistrate, and by 21 & 22 *Vic.* c. 73, a stipendiary magistrate, may act in the same way.

The summary power given by this section does not prevent proceedings by indictment, although the offender is a member of the society, *Rex* v. *Hall*, 1 Moody Cr. Cas. 474; nor take away the common law remedy by action, *Sharpe* v. *Warren*, 6 Price 131; *Sinden* v. *Banks*, 30 L. J. (Q. B.) 102. Trespass will not lie against a magistrate for anything done by him under this section, unless he is made acquainted with every fact necessary to enable him to determine when called on to act; as, for instance, where the rules directed disputes to be referred to arbitration, *Pike* v. *Carter,* 10 Moore 376.

The 12th section of the 4 & 5 *W.* 4. c. 40, giving priority of payment of debts, in case of any officer appointed to any office in the society, who may have in his hands, by virtue of his office or employment, any monies of the society, dying or becoming bankrupt or insolvent, &c., applies only to cases of debts in respect of money received by officers by virtue of their office, and independent of contract. Thus it was held, upon the construction of the 10th section of the 33 *Geo.* 3. c. 54 (similar to this section), that the section did not apply to debts due from officers individually, and not in their official characters : *Ex parte The Amicable Society of Lancaster,* 6 Vesey 98, nor to money held by a person not appointed treasurer, or by the treasurer upon notes carrying interest; *Ashley, Ex parte,* 6 Ves. 441 ; *Ross, Ex parte,* ib. 802 ; *Stamford Friendly Society, Ex parte,* 15 Ves. 280 ; and see *Buckland, Ex parte,* 1 Buck. 514, *Anon.* 6 Mad. 98 ; nor to bankers appointed to receive money and remit to their London agent for the purpose of investment, *Ex parte Whipham,* 3 Mont. D. & D. 564 ; *Harris, Ex parte,* 1 De Gex 162. But where the bankrupt, on being appointed treasurer, was by the rules to pay interest on the amount in his hand, it was held that the section applied, as being money in his hands by virtue of his office as treasurer, and that the assignees were liable to pay over the amount to the society, *Ray, Ex parte,* 1 M. & Ch. 537 ; and where the treasurer of a savings bank was partner in a bank into which all monies received by the manager were paid to the credit of the trustees, and interest allowed thereon, and the treasurer acknowledged from time to time the balance to be monies in his hands as treasurer, held, under a similar clause in a Savings Bank Act to that now under consideration, that such balance was to be deemed as in his hands as treasurer at the time of his bankruptcy, and the trustees entitled to recover the amount in full, *Riddell, Ex parte,* 3 Mont. D. & D. 80.   In the case, however, of *Ex parte Jardine,* 10 Law Jour. N. S. (B.) 11, 1 Fonblanque 324, it was held that an actuary of a savings bank, who by the rules had no power to receive money, but was allowed to do so by the manager, could not be said to have received it by virtue of his office, and therefore that the trustees of the bank had no priority over the other creditors. Where a joint fiat in bankruptcy was issued against the treasurer of a savings bank and his co-partner, it was held, under the clause in the Savings Bank Act, that the bank could only claim a priority of payment in respect of monies due from the treasurer out of his separate estate, and that they had no claim against the joint estate, although the separate estate was not sufficient to pay the whole amount, *Ex parte Appach,* 1 Mont. D. & D. 83.

A treasurer of a Friendly Society took a security in the name of the society from a debtor of his own, retained the amount of his debt out of the society's money, afterwards debited himself annually in the society's accounts with the interest of the amount for which the security was taken, and then became bankrupt. The security proving insufficient, and not being a security within the Friendly Societies Acts, it was held that the society was not deprived of the right of priority of payment by reason of not having taken steps to set aside the transaction, or to realise the security before the bankruptcy, *Ex parte Burge*, 1 Mont. D. & D. 540.

The Act does not provide for the case of a person *employed* in any office, but only of one appointed to an office; so where no bankers were appointed, but the money of the society was paid into a bank, it was held that the society was not entitled to priority, *Orford, Ex parte*, 1 De Gex, M. & G. 483.

The circumstance of the society not having audited the accounts of their treasurer was held not to deprive them of their priority, and it was also held that the filing and service of a Bill by the trustees to enforce such priority was a demand in writing within the meaning of the Act, *Absalum v. Gethin*, 11 Weekly Rep. 332.

Where a society had authorised two of the trustees and a director to borrow money from the bankers of the society upon their joint and several promissory note, and the bankers at the time of their bankruptcy held the note, and there was also a balance in their hands to the credit of the society upon its current account, it was held that the society was entitled to set off the amount of its balance against the sum due upon the note, *Clennell, Ex parte*, 9 Weekly Rep. 380.

The trustees and secretary of a society were held personally responsible for a promissory note signed by them for money lent to the society, *Price* v. *Taylor*, 8 Weekly Rep. 419; *Bottomley* v. *Fisher*, 10 Weekly Rep. 668; and where by the rules of the society the surveyor was to be paid out of the funds, the committee were held liable, although the purpose for which he was employed was not within the objects of the society as the building of houses, *Alexander* v. *Worman*, 30 Law J. (Exc.) 199.

The society is liable for necessary work although the order for the same is not given in the manner directed by the rules, *Atlard* v. *Bourne*, 15 Com. Bench Rep. 468.

Great strictness must be observed in following the rules as to the appointment of officers. In the case of *Roberts* v. *Price*, 4 C. B. Rep. 231, the rules vested in a committee of eleven the power of electing a treasurer and other officers. At a meeting of the committee when ten only were present, the eleventh not having received notice, the former treasurer was removed and another person appointed in his stead by a majority of votes. But it was held that the election was void, although the absent committeeman had for a considerable period ceased to attend the meetings, and had intimated an intention of not attending again, and although the former treasurer had demanded a poll.

In *R.* v. *Oldham and the United Insurance Society*, 15 Jurist 1035, it was decided that the officers of a Friendly Society were bound, under section 9 of 10 *Geo.* 4. c. 56, to sign a notice to convene a general meeting of the members, upon a requisition for that purpose being duly made to them.

Where notice of the holding of a meeting has been properly given, there is no necessity for giving notice of its bonâ fide adjournment, *Kerr* v. *Wilkie*, 8 Weekly Rep. 286.

PART III.

RIGHTS AND LIABILITIES OF MEMBERS.

Individuals only, and not persons forming a Joint Stock Company, can be members of these societies, *Dobinson* v. *Hawkes*, 16 Sim. 407 ; and although by the 32nd sec. of the 10 *Geo.* 4. c. 56, minors may be members of Friendly Societies, and execute all instruments, and give all necessary acquittances, and enjoy all privileges, yet it is conceived that this section is not applicable to Benefit Building Societies, as minors clearly cannot execute deeds or transfers.

A member cannot refuse to pay his subscriptions on account of the misapplication of the funds of the society, such as their being laid out in the purchase of land to be allotted among the members, *Hughes* v. *D'Eyncourt*, 12 Weekly Rep. 408, 10 Jur. 513 ; and a borrowing member may still be liable to pay his subscriptions, although entitled by the rules to receive back his deeds with a receipt endorsed upon the security, *Farmer* v. *Giles*, 30 Law J. (Exc.) 65 ; *Farmer* v. *Smith*, 28 Law J. (Exc.) 226.

In these cases it appeared that, by the rules of
a Benefit Building Society, every shareholder paying 10*s*. a month on each share, was entitled to
receive out of the funds a stated sum, in advance
and satisfaction on each share towards the purchase
of land, viz., 60*l*. if advanced during the first year,
and increasing to 120*l*. in the thirteenth year; and
on the other hand, shareholders not receiving an
advance were, on withdrawing from the society,
entitled to a sum commencing with 6*l*. if withdrawing at the end of the first year, and increasing to 120*l*. if withdrawing at the end of the
thirteenth year. Each shareholder receiving an
advance was required to execute to the society a
mortgage of the land, with a covenant to pay the
subscriptions on his shares according to the rules of
the society; but each shareholder might at any
time satisfy the security by paying the subscriptions to the end of the thirteenth year of the society's existence, and was thereupon entitled to a
receipt by the trustees of the society (indorsed on
the mortgage pursuant to section 5 of the 6 and 7
Will. 4. c. 32), for all monies intended to be secured
by the deed. The rules stipulated that the society
should terminate when the sum of 120*l*. for each
unadvanced share, with all other expenses and liabilities of the society, should be fully realised; and
that the subscription of 10*s*. a month should continue to be paid until the objects of the society should
be fully accomplished; and it was held, that although
the society contemplated that at the end of the thirteenth year, at the furthest, all its objects would

be accomplished; yet that as, in consequence of want of funds, such objects were not effected in that time, the shareholders continued liable to the payment of their subscriptions. And also, that although a shareholder, having received an advance and executed a mortgage, was entitled at any time before the termination of the thirteen years to redeem the mortgage by payment of the subscriptions to the thirteenth year, and although the receipt indorsed on the deed vested the estate in him, such redemption did not operate to discharge him from the covenant to pay the subscriptions according to the rules; and consequently, that he continued liable to the subscriptions after the thirteen years, as the objects of the society were not accomplished. This decision was followed by the Master of the Rolls in the case of *Sparrow* v. *Farmer*, 28 Law J. (Ch.) 537.

Where, however, the rules expressly empowered the managers to determine the amount of money to be paid by any mortgagor in full for the claims of the society upon his property, on payment of which, the share or shares in respect of which the security was made were to be wholly extinguished, it was held that the payment of the sum fixed by the managers, and the receipt indorsed upon the mortgage, was a total extinguishment of the shares, and that the member was not liable to pay any further subscriptions, *Priestly* v. *Hopwood*, 12 Weekly Rep. 1031.

The question which has given rise to the greatest discussion is as to the terms upon which the mortgagor is entitled to redeem his property, and this depends, of course, upon the rules and the mortgage deed.   In *Mosley v. Baker*, 6 Hare 87, by the rules of the society 10s. a month subscription and 4s. a month redemption monies were payable on each advanced share, until a sum of 120l. per share should be realised for the non-purchasing members ; and any member might redeem by paying the full amount expressed to be secured by the mortgage, deducting the amount of the subscriptions paid by him, and the profits of his shares up to that time. Any member, upon withdrawal, was to receive back his subscriptions, subject to a fine of so much per share ; but after the fifth year of the society he was also entitled to receive such a bonus as the directors might determine.   The mortgage was expressed to be made for securing the payments of the subscriptions, redemption, and other monies payable in respect of the shares according to the rules, and it declared that upon a sale under the power of sale all monies which should at any time afterwards become due should be considered as due at the time of the sale, and that out of the proceeds of the sale there was to be retained all subscriptions then and to be thereafter due, calculating the probable duration of the society ; and it was held in a redemption suit, before the fifth year of the society, that the member could redeem only upon payment of all the future subscriptions on his shares until the dissolution of the society, the *probable* duration to be ascertained by calculation, and the future payments to be treated as if immediately due, and this decision was affirmed on appeal, *S. C.* 3 De Gex, M. & G. 1033

The next case, *Seagrave* v. *Pope*, 1 De Gex, Mac. & Gordon 193, where the facts were very much the same as in the previous case, was decided in the same way.

The next case which came before the Courts was that of *Fleming* v. *Self*, 3 De Gex, Mac. & Gordon 997.   In that case the rules and mortgage deed were very similar to those in the other cases, but the society had existed more than five years, and in the mortgage deed there was no provision as to calculating the probable duration of the society in the event of a sale under the deed ; and a decree was made for redemption, directing calculation to be made of the longest possible duration of the society at the date of the notice to redeem, having regard to the net assets of the society, and to the monthly subscriptions and redemption money still continuing payable, and the number of 120*l.* shares to be provided for, and charging the member as a present debt with all subscriptions and redemption money which would become payable by him, assuming the society to endure for the whole of the calculated period, and crediting him with the amount of bonus payable at the date of the notice to withdrawing members.

The decree in the last case was in *Smith* v. *Pilkington*, 1 De Gex, F. & J., a case on the same rules, held binding, and also that it extended to the deduction of redemption monies paid in by the mortgagor, although that point was not expressly referred to in the judgment in that case.

No alterations of rules or new rules are binding

upon the members who have previously given notice of withdrawal, *Armitage* v. *Walker*, 2 Kay & John. 211.

A member upon withdrawing from the society is always entitled by the rules to receive back the amount of his subscriptions, generally with interest, and also a share of profits. By the rules of a society the directors were authorised to invest the funds on mortgage for ten years at interest, or in building on or improving land mortgaged to them, and members might withdraw upon giving a certain notice, but no time was specified for making the payments they were to receive, and the directors had power to pay such claims in the order in which they arose ; and it was held that it was competent to the arbitrator to consider when, consistently with the due prosecution of the other objects of the society, such payment should be made, and to fix a time accordingly, *Armitage* v. *Walker, supra.*

The only other point relating to the rights of members to be referred to is, the right of a borrowing member in possession of the mortgaged premises under the mortgaged deed to be registered as a county voter. It has been held that where the payments to be made do not reduce the annual value below 40s., then the member has a right to be so registered. In *Robinson, app.* v. *Derby, resp.* 12 W. Rep. 202, it appeared that the society some years ago had advanced to the member 73l., and that the monthly repayments amounted to 4l. per annum; the claimant had paid 71l. before January 1863, and the whole purchase of 73l. was completed

by the payment of the remaining 2*l.* in July 1863.
The revising barrister was of opinion that the claimant was progressing towards the acquisition of his
freehold, which, when fully paid up, would have cost
him 73*l.*, of which he had paid 71*l.* before January
1863, and found that he had a freehold prior to the
31st of January last of the value of 40*l.* per annum,
and therefore he retained his vote, and the Court
were of opinion that the revising barrister was right.
The difficulty in this case arose entirely from the
decision in the case of *Copeland* v. *Bartlett,* 26 Com.
Bench Rep. 662 ; the circumstances of the case were
nearly identical, but the barrister did not find the
value of the claimant's beneficial interest, and therefore his interest did not appear to be of the value
of 40*s.*

PART IV.

SETTLEMENT OF DISPUTES.

The 27th sec. of the 10 *Geo.* 4. c. 56, directs provision to be made in the rules for the settlement of
disputes, and this direction has been repeatedly held
to exclude the jurisdiction of the Superior Courts,
see *Ex parte Payne,* 5 Dow. and L. 679 ; *Reeves* v.
White, 18 Justice of the Peace 118 ; *Grinham* v.
Card, 7 Exc. Repts. 833. In *Armitage* v. *Walker,*
2 Kay and J. 211, it was held that neither a Court
of Law nor Equity could alter the award of arbitrators or justices unless there was error upon the

face of it, or it was shown to have been corruptly obtained.

The dispute, however, must be one between the society and a member as a member, and not in any other capacity he may fill as a mortgagor, &c. : see *Morrison* v. *Glover*, 19 L. J. Rep. (Exc.) 20, where the member was sued upon his covenant in the mortgage deed ; *Farmer* v. *Giles*, 30 L. J. (Exc.) 65, which was an action upon the covenant in the mortgage deed for payment of the subscriptions, &c. ; *Harmer* v. *Gooding*, 13 Jur. 400 ; *Smith* v. *Lloyd*, 26 Beav. 507, suits for an account and a dissolution of the society ; *Fleming* v. *Self*, 3 De Gex, M. and G., a redemption suit.

The dispute is by the Act to be between the society and any individual member thereof, or person claiming on account of any member, and in *Knox* v. *Shephard*, 36 Law Times 351, it was held that where the administrators of a deceased member had been treated by the society as a member, the rule as to the settlement of disputes applied to him. The Act provides for the nomination of new arbitrators in case of the death or refusal to act of the former ones ; and in *Re Evans*, 18 Justice of the Peace 247, where the arbitrators appointed by the rules were superseded by mistake, and new ones were bonâ fide appointed in the belief that the former were dead or had refused to act, it was held that an award made by the newly-appointed arbitrators was valid. The award must be made according to the true purport and meaning of the rules, to be valid and binding ; therefore, where by the rules the arbitrators were to hear evidence on both sides, it was held that as they had refused to hear evidence on the part of the member the award was bad, *Re Grant*, 14 Q.B. Rep. 43; it is clear, however, that they may decline to hear counsel, *In re Macqueen*, 9 Com. Bench Rep. N. S. 793.

The award may be enforced by any one justice, who may issue a warrant of distress for the money awarded if not immediately paid, and it was held, in *Hammond* v. *Bendyshe*, 13 Q.B. Repts. 872, that a previous summons to show cause against such issuing is not necessary. All that the magistrate has to see is, that the rules of the society have been properly certified, and the award properly made, *Hughes* v. *D'Eyncourt*, 12 W. R. 409. By the 28th section of the 10 *Geo.* 4. c. 56, justices may decide disputes if the rules so direct; and by section 7 of 4 and 5 *Will.* 4. c. 40, if no award shall have been made by the arbitrators within forty days after application to the society, justices may decide the dispute; and by the next section power is given to justices, and also to the arbitrators, to order an expelled member to be reinstated, or in default of reinstatement they may award to the member a sum of money as compensation, to be recoverable from the society in the same way as any money awarded by arbitrators is recoverable. Before, however, a distress warrant is issued for non-compliance with any order made under these sections directing money to be paid, a previous summons to the party is necessary, to show cause against the issuing of the warrant, *Hammond* v. *Bendyshe*, 13 Q.B. Rep. 872. The jurisdiction of the justice must be confined strictly to the subject-matter of complaint, as was held in *Rex* v. *Soper*, 3 Barn. & Cr. 857, where it appeared that on the complaint of an expelled member of a Friendly Society of having been deprived of relief to which he was entitled, the justices awarded not only that the steward should give him such relief, *but also that he should be continued a member of the society*; and it was held that the latter part of the order was illegal, inasmuch as the expulsion of the party was no part of the complaint. Every material fact to show the jurisdiction of the justices must be set forth in the order. See *Day* v. *King*, 5 Ad. & Ell. 359. It was decided in *Rex* v. *Wade*, 1 Barn. & Ad. 861, that an indictment lay against the president and stewards of a Friendly Society for disobeying an order of justices addressed to them, to readmit a member, though it was sworn that the power of doing so was not in them, but in a committee; and in *Rex* v. *Gash*, 1 Starkie 441, where, upon a complaint made by an excluded member, the then stewards were summoned, and an order was made that they and other members of the society should reinstate the complainant, the order was served on the stewards after they had ceased to be so, but it was held that it was still obligatory upon them as members to attempt to reinstate the complainant, and that their having ceased to be stewards was no justification of entire neglect on their part. On an indictment against the officers of a Friendly Society for not re-admitting a member on the order of justices, it was held to be no defence that the party was not eligible to be a member by the rules, as that was matter of defence before the justices, *Rex* v. *Gilkes*, 2 Car. & P. 52.

Where the trustees had expelled a member, it was held upon an application for a mandamus to reinstate him, that the question was one for settlement under the rules, *Woolrich, Ex parte*, 31 Law J. (Q.B.) 122.*

PART V.

STAMPS.

Under the provisions of the 37th section of the 10 *Geo.* 4. c. 56, and the 8th section of the 6 & 7 *Wm.* 4. c. 32, mortgages and other securities to Benefit Building Societies are exempt from stamp duty, *Walker* v. *Giles*, 6 Com. Bench Rep. 662 ; *Barnard* v. *Pilsworth*, Ib. 698. In both these cases it was held that, reading the 37th section as incorporated into the Benefit Building Societies Act, so far as applicable it exempted from stamp duty all securities given for the purpose of carrying that Act into effect; and further, that a later Act limiting the exemption previously given to Friendly Societies did not affect the Building Societies Act, which was an independent statute. These societies, by virtue of the above sections, are exempt from the duty on

---

* The remarks at p. 10, as to the time within which the complaint must be made, and as to the jurisdiction of the lord mayor, aldermen, police and stipendiary magistrates, apply to these sections.

draughts or orders, imposed by the 21 & 22 *Vic.* c. 20.

Upon the construction of a similar clause to the above in a former Act, it was held that a bond conditioned for the production of a box containing the subscriptions of a society was free from stamp duty, *Carter* v. *Bond,* 4 Exp. 235.

6 & 7 WILL. 4, CAP. 32.

An Act for the Regulation of Benefit Building Societies. [14th July 1836.]

Whereas certain societies commonly called building societies have been established in different parts of the kingdom, principally amongst the industrious classes, for the purpose of raising by small periodical subscriptions a fund to assist the members thereof in obtaining a small freehold or leasehold property, and it is expedient to afford encouragement and protection to such societies and the property obtained therewith : Be it therefore enacted by the King's most excellent Majesty, by and with the advice and consent of the lords spiritual and temporal, and commons, in this present parliament assembled, and by the authority of the same, That it shall and may be lawful for any number of persons in Great Britain and Ireland to form themselves into and establish societies for the purpose of raising, by the monthly or other subscriptions of the several members of such societies, shares not exceeding the value of one hundred and fifty pounds * for each share, such subscriptions not to exceed in the whole twenty shillings per month for each share, a stock or fund for the purpose of enabling each member thereof to receive out of the funds of such society the amount or value of his or her share or shares therein, to erect or purchase one or more dwelling-house or dwelling-houses, or other real or leasehold estate to be secured by way of mortgage to such society until the amount or value of his or her shares shall have been fully repaid to such society with the interest thereon, and all fines or other payments incurred in respect thereof, and to and for the several members of each society from time to time to assemble together, and to make, ordain, and constitute such proper and wholesome rules and regulations for the government and guidance

Societies may be established for the purchase or erection of dwelling-houses.

* A member may hold any number of shares notwithstanding this limit, Morrison *v.* Glover, 19 L. J. (Exc.) 20.

c 2

of the same as to the major part of the members of such society so assembled together shall seem meet, so as such rules shall not be repugnant to the express provisions of this Act and to the general laws of the realm, and to impose and inflict such reasonable fines, penalties, and forfeitures upon the several members of any such society who shall offend against any such rules, as the members may think fit, to be respectively paid to such uses for the benefit of such society as such society by such rules shall direct, and also from time to time to alter and amend such rules as occasion shall require, or annul or repeal the same, and to make new rules in lieu thereof, under such restrictions as are in this Act contained ; provided that no member shall receive or be entitled to receive from the funds of such society any interest or dividend, by way of annual or other periodical profit upon any shares in such society, until the amount or value of his or her share shall have been realized, except on the withdrawal of such member, according to the rules of such society then in force.

Bonus, &c. not to be usurious. II. And be it enacted, That it shall and may be lawful to and for any such society to have and receive from any member or members thereof any sum or sums of money, by way of bonus on any share or shares, for the privilege of receiving the same in advance prior to the same being realized, and also any interest for the share or shares so received or any part thereof, without being subject or liable on account thereof to any of the forfeitures or penalties imposed by any Act or Acts of Parliament relating to usury.

Rules may be made to provide forms of conveyance, &c. III. And be it further enacted, That it shall and may be lawful to and for any such society, in and by the rules thereof, to describe the form or forms of conveyance, mortgage, transfer, agreement, bond, or other instrument which may be necessary for carrying the purposes of the said society into execution ; and which shall be specified and set forth in a schedule to be annexed to the rules of such society, and duly certified and deposited as hereinafter provided.

Provisions of Friendly Society Acts of 10 Geo. 4, c. 56, and 4 & 5 W. 4, c. 40, extended to this Act. IV. And be it further enacted, That all the provisions of a certain Act made and passed in the tenth year of the reign of His late Majesty King George the Fourth, intituled an Act to consolidate and amend the laws relating to friendly societies, and also the provisions of a certain other Act made and passed in the fourth and fifth years of the reign of His present

Majesty King William the Fourth, intituled an Act
to amend an Act of the tenth year of His late Majesty
King George the Fourth, to consolidate and amend
the laws relating to friendly societies, so far as the
same, or any part thereof, may be applicable to the
purpose of any benefit building society, and to the
framing, certifying, enrolling, and altering the rules
thereof, shall extend and apply to such benefit building society and the rules thereof in such and the same
manner as if the provisions of the said Acts had been
herein expressly re-enacted.

V. And be it further enacted, That it shall be
lawful for the trustees named in any mortgage made
on behalf of such societies, or the survivor or survivors of them, or for the trustees for the time being,
to endorse upon any mortgage or further charge given
by any member of such society to the trustees thereof
for monies advanced by such society to any member
thereof, a receipt for all monies intended to be secured
by such mortgage or further charge, which shall be
sufficient to vacate the same, and vest the estate of
and in the property comprised in such security in the
person or persons for the time being entitled to the
equity of redemption, without it being necessary for
the trustees of any such society to give any re-conveyance of the property so mortgaged, which receipt shall
be specified in a schedule to be annexed to the rules of
such society, duly certified and deposited as afore-
said. *(Receipt endorsed on mortgage to be sufficient discharge without re-conveyance.)*

VI. Provided always, and be it further enacted,
That nothing herein contained shall authorize any
benefit building society to invest its funds, or any
part thereof, in any savings bank, or with the com-
missioners for the reduction of the national debt. *(Not to authorise investment of funds in Savings Bank.)*

VII. And be it further enacted, That all building
societies established prior to the first day of June
one thousand eight hundred and thirty six shall be
entitled to the protection and benefits of this Act,
on their present rules being duly certified and deposited as directed by the said recited Acts; and no
such society shall be entitled to the benefits of this
Act until their rules shall have been so certified and
deposited; and that no such society shall be required
to alter in any manner the rules under which they
are now respectively governed. *(Benefit of Act to extend to all societies established prior to June 1836.)*

VIII. And be it further enacted, That no rules of
any such society, or any copy thereof, nor any transfer
of any share or shares in any such society, shall be *(Exemption from stamp duties.)*

subject or liable to or charged with any stamp duty or duties whatsoever.

Public Act.   IX. And be it further enacted, That this Act shall be deemed a public Act, and shall extend to Great Britain, Ireland, and Berwick-upon-Tweed, and be judicially taken notice of as such by all judges, justices, and other persons whatsoever, without the same being specially shown or pleaded.

---

10 GEO. 4, CAP. 56.

An Act to consolidate and amend the Laws relating to Friendly Societies.   [*19th June* 1829.]

I. [This section repeals the former Acts relating to friendly societies.]

II. [This section authorizes the establishment of friendly societies.]

Societies in their rules, to declare the purpose of their establishment, &c.   III. And be it further enacted, That every such society so to be established as aforesaid, before any of the rules thereof shall be confirmed by the justices in the manner hereinafter directed, shall, in or by one more of the rules to be confirmed by such justices, declare all and every the intents and purposes for which such society is intended to be established, and shall also in and by such rules direct all and every the uses and purposes to which the money which shall from time to time be subscribed, paid, or given to or for the use or benefit of such society, or which shall arise therefrom, or in anywise shall belong to such society, shall be appropriated and applied, and in what shares and proportions and under what circumstances any member of such society, or other person, shall or may become entitled to the same or any part thereof; provided that the application thereof shall not in anywise be repugnant to the uses, intents, and purposes of such society, or any of them, so to be declared as aforesaid; and all such rules, during the continuance of the same, shall be complied with and enforced; and the monies so subscribed, paid, or given, or so arising, to or for the use or benefit of such society, or belonging thereto, shall not be diverted or misapplied either by the treasurer, trustee, or any other officer or member of such society entrusted therewith, under such penalty or forfeiture as such society shall by any rule impose and inflict for such offence.

IV. [This section, which set forth the manner in which the rules of a society were to be certified, is repealed by 4 and 5 W. 4, cap. 40, sec. 4 *infra.*]

V. Provided always, and be it further enacted, That in case any such barrister or advocate shall refuse to certify all or any of the rules so to be submitted for his perusal and examination, it shall then be lawful for any such society to submit the same to the court of quarter sessions, together with the reasons assigned by the said barrister or advocate, in writing, for any such rejection or disapproval of any one or more such rules; and that the justices at their said quarter sessions shall and may, if they think fit, confirm and allow the same, notwithstanding any such rejection or disapproval by any such barrister or advocate.

Manner of proceeding in case barrister shall refuse to certify.

VI. [This section relates to the tables of friendly societies.]

VII. And be it further enacted, That no such society as aforesaid shall have the benefit of this Act, unless all the rules for the management thereof shall be entered in a book to be kept by an officer of such society appointed for that purpose, and which book shall be open at all seasonable times for the inspection of the members of such society, and unless all such rules shall be fairly transcribed, and such transcript deposited with the clerk of the peace for the county wherein such society shall be established as aforesaid; but nevertheless nothing contained herein shall extend to prevent any alteration in or amendment of any such rules so entered and deposited and filed as aforesaid, or repealing or annulling the same, or any of them, in the whole or in part, or making any new rules for the management of such society, in such manner as by the rules of such society shall from time to time be provided; but such new rules, or such alterations in or amendments of former rules, or any order annulling or repealing any former rules in the whole or in part, shall not be in force until the same respectively shall be entered in such book as aforesaid, and certified, when necessary, by such barrister or advocate as aforesaid, and until a transcript thereof shall be deposited with such clerk of the peace as aforesaid, who shall file and certify the same as aforesaid; *and that no such rule, or alteration in or amendment of any former rule, shall be binding or have*

No society entitled to the benefit of this Act, unless their rules have been confirmed.

*any force or effect until the same shall have been con-
firmed by such justices, and filed as aforesaid.*

Rules, when entered and deposited, to be binding on members and depositors.

VIII. And be it further enacted, That all rules from time to time made and in force for the management of such society as aforesaid, and duly entered in such book as aforesaid, and confirmed by the justices as aforesaid, shall be binding on the several members and officers of such society, and the several contributors thereto, and their representatives, all of whom shall be deemed and taken to have full notice thereof by such entry and contribution as aforesaid ; and the entry of such rules in such book as aforesaid, or the

Copy of transcript to be received in evidence.

transcript thereof deposited with such clerk of the peace as aforesaid, or a true copy of such transcript, examined with the original and proved to be a true copy, shall be received as evidence of such rules respectively in all cases ; and no certiorari, suspension, advocation, reduction, or other legal process shall be brought or allowed to remove any such rules into any of His Majesty's courts of record ; and every copy of any such transcript deposited with any clerk of the peace as aforesaid shall be made without fee or reward, except the actual expense of making such copy.

No confirmed rule to be altered but at a general meeting of the society, &c.

IX. And be it further enacted, That no rule confirmed by the justices of the peace in manner aforesaid shall be altered, rescinded, or repealed, unless at a general meeting of the members of such society as aforesaid, convened by public notice, written or printed, signed by the secretary or president or other principal officer or clerk of such society, in pursuance of a requisition for that purpose by seven or more of the members of such society, which said requisition and notice shall be publicly read at the two usual meetings of such society to be held next before such general meeting for the purpose of such alteration or repeal, unless a committee of such members shall have been nominated for that purpose at a general meeting of the members of such society convened in manner aforesaid, in which case such committee shall have the like power to make such alterations or repeal, and unless such alterations or repeal shall be made with the concurrence and approbation of three-fourths of the members of such society then and there present, or by the like proportion of such committee

* The words in *italics* are repealed by 4 and 5 W. 4, cap. 40, s. 4 *infra.*

as aforesaid, if any shall have been nominated for that purpose.

X. And be it further enacted, That the rules of every society formed under the authority of this Act shall specify the place or places at which it is intended such society shall hold its meetings, and shall contain provisions with respect to the powers and duties of the members at large, and of such committees or officers as may be appointed for the management of the affairs of such society ; provided always, that it shall and may be lawful for any such society to alter their place or places of meeting whenever they may consider it necessary, upon giving notice thereof in writing to the clerk of the peace for the county within which such society shall be held, the said notice to be given within seven days before or after such removal, and signed by the secretary or other principal officer, and also by three or more of the members of the said society ; and provided that the place or places at which such society intend to hold their meetings shall be situate within the county in which the rules of the said society are enrolled.

XI. And be it further enacted, That every such society shall and may from time to time, at any of their usual meetings, or by their committee, if any such shall be appointed for that society, elect and appoint such person into the office of steward, president, warden, treasurer, or trustee of such society, as they shall think proper, and also shall and may from time to time elect and appoint such clerks and other officers as shall be deemed necessary to carry into execution the purposes of such society, for such space of time and for such purposes as shall be fixed and established by the rules of such society, and from time to time to elect and appoint others in the room of those who shall vacate or die ; and such treasurer, trustee, and all and every other officer or other person whatever who shall be appointed to any office in anywise touching or concerning the receipt, management, or expenditure of any sum of money collected for the purpose of any such society, before he, she, or they shall be admitted to take upon him, her, or them the execution of any such office or trust, (if required so to do by the rules of such society to which such officer shall belong,) shall become bound in a bond, according to the form prescribed in the schedule to this Act annexed, with two sufficient sureties, for the just and faithful execution of such office or trust, and

Rules shall specify place of meeting and duties of officers.

Societies may alter place of meeting.

Society may appoint officers.

Securities to be given for offices of trust, if required.

for rendering a just and true account according to the rules of such society, and in all matters lawful to pay obedience to the same, in such penal sum of money as by the major part of such society at any such meeting as aforesaid shall be thought expedient, and to the

Treasurer or trustees to give bond to clerk of the peace.

satisfaction of such society; and that every such bond to be given by or on the behalf of such treasurer or trustee, or of any other person appointed to any other office or trust, shall be given to the clerk of the peace of the county where such society shall be established, for the time being, without fee or reward; and in case of forfeiture it shall be lawful to sue upon such bond in the name of the clerk of the peace for the time being, for the use of the said society, fully indemnifying and saving harmless such clerk of the peace from all costs and charges in respect of such suit; provided that such bond shall have in Scotland the same force and effect as a bond in the form in use in Scotland containing a clause of registration.

Appointment of committees.

XII. And be it further enacted, That every such society shall and may from time to time elect and appoint any number of the members of such society to be a committee, the number thereof to be declared in the rules of every such society, and shall and may delegate to such committee all or any of the powers given by this Act to be executed, who, being so delegated, shall continue to act as such committee, for and during such time as they shall be appointed, for

Powers of standing committees to be declared in the rules of the society, and of particular ones entered in a book.

such society, for general purposes, the powers of such committee being first declared in and by the rules of such society, confirmed by the justices of the peace at their sessions, and filed in the manner hereinbefore directed; and in all cases where a committee shall be appointed for any particular purpose, the powers delegated to such committee shall be reduced into writing, and entered into a book by the secretary or clerk of such society, and a majority of the members of such committee shall at all times be necessary to concur in any Act of such committee; and such committee shall, in all things delegated to them, act for and in the name of such society; and all acts and orders of such committee, under the powers delegated to them, shall have the like force and effect as the acts and orders of such society at any general meeting thereof could or might have had in pursuance of this Act:

Committee controllable by society.

Provided always, that the transactions of such committee shall be entered in a book belonging to such society, and shall be from time to time and at all times subject and liable to the review, allowance, or disallowance and control of such society, in such manner and form as such society shall by their general rules, confirmed by the justices and filed as aforesaid, have directed and appointed, or shall in like manner direct and appoint.

XIII. And be it further enacted, That it shall and may be lawful to and for the treasurer or trustee for the time being of any such society, and he, she, and they is and are hereby authorized and required, from time to time, by and with the consent of such society, to be had and testified in such manner as shall be directed by the general rules of such society, to lay out or dispose of such part of all such sums of money as shall at any time be collected, given, or paid to and for the beneficial ends, intents, and purposes of such society, as the exigencies of such society shall not call for the immediate application or expenditure of, either on real or heritable securities or heritable property, to be approved of as aforesaid, (such securities to be taken in the name of such treasurer or trustee for the time being,) or to invest the same in the public stocks or funds, savings banks,* or government securities, or in any of the chartered banks in Scotland, or in the bank of the Commercial Banking Company of Scotland, and not otherwise, in the proper name of such treasurer or trustee; and from time to time, with such consent as aforesaid, to alter and transfer such securities and funds, and to make sale thereof respectively; and that all the dividends, interests, and proceeds which shall from to time arise from the monies so laid out or invested as aforesaid shall from time to time be brought to account by such treasurer or trustee, and shall be applied to and for the use of such society, according to the rules thereof.

XIV. And be it further enacted, That every person who shall have or receive any part of the monies, effects, or funds of or belonging to any such society, or shall in any manner have been or shall be entrusted with the disposal, management, or custody thereof, or of any securities, books, papers, or property relating to the same, his or her executors, administrators, and assigns respectively, shall, upon demand made, or notice in writing given or left at the last or usual place of residence of such persons, in pursuance of any

Marginal notes: Treasurer or trustee to lay out surplus of contributions; and to bring the proceeds to account. Treasurer, &c. to render accounts, and pay over balances, &c.

* This investment is prohibited by 6 and 7 W. 4, c. 32, s. 6 *supra.*

order of such society, or committee to be appointed as aforesaid, for that purpose, give in his or her account at the usual meeting of such society, or to such committee thereof as aforesaid, to be examined and allowed or disallowed by such society or committee thereof, and shall, on the like demand or notice, pay over all the monies remaining in his or her hands, and assign and transfer or deliver all securities and effects, books, papers, and property, taken or standing in his or her name as aforesaid, or being in his or her hands or custody, to the treasurer or trustee for the time being, or to such other person as such society or committee thereof shall appoint; and

and in case of neglect, application may be made to the Court of Exchequer, &c.

in case of any neglect or refusal to deliver such account, or to pay over such monies, or to assign, transfer, or deliver such securities and effects, books, papers, and property in manner aforesaid, it shall and may be lawful to and for every such society, in the name of the treasurer or trustee or other principal officer thereof, as the case may be, to exhibit a petition in the Court of Exchequer * in England or Ireland, or in the Court of Session in Scotland, or the courts of great sessions in Wales respectively, who shall and may proceed thereupon in a summary way, and make such order therein, upon hearing all parties concerned, as to such court in their discretion shall seem just, which order shall be final and conclusive ; and all assignments, sales, and transfers made in pursuance of such order shall be good and effectual in law to all intents and purposes whatsoever.

Where trustees, &c. are out of jurisdiction of court, or it be uncertain whether they are alive, or they refuse to convey, &c. Court of Exchequer may appoint a person to convey.

XV. And be it further enacted, That when and so often as any person seised or possessed of any lands, tenements, or hereditaments, or other property, or any estate or interest therein, as a trustee of any such society, shall be out of the jurisdiction of or not amenable to the process of the Court of Exchequer * in England or Ireland, or the Court of Session in Scotland, or of the courts of great sessions in Wales, or shall be idiot, lunatic, or of unsound mind, or it shall be unknown or uncertain whether he or she be living or dead, or such person shall refuse to convey or otherwise assure such lands, tenements, hereditaments, or property, or estate or interest, to the person duly nominated as trustee of such society in their stead, either alone or together with any continuing trustee, as occasion shall require, then and in every or any

* Now the Court of Chancery.

such case it shall be lawful for the judges of the said
courts respectively to appoint such person, as to such
court shall seem meet, on behalf and in the name of
the person seised or possessed as aforesaid, to convey,
surrender, release, assign, or otherwise assure the said
lands, tenements, hereditaments, or property, or estate
or interest, to such trustee so duly nominated as
aforesaid; and every such conveyance, release, surrender, assignment, or assurance shall be as valid and
effectual to all intents and purposes as if the person
being out of the jurisdiction or not amenable to the
process of the said courts, or not known to be alive,
or having refused, or as if the person being idiot,
lunatic, or of unsound mind, had been at the time of
the execution thereof of sane mind, memory, and
understanding, and had by himself or herself executed
the same.

XVI. And be it further enacted, That when and as
often as it shall happen that all and every person in
whose name any part of the several stocks, annuities,
and funds transferable or which hereafter shall be
made transferable at the Bank of England, or in the
books of the governor and company of the Bank of
England, is, are, or shall be standing as a trustee of
any such society, shall be absent, out of the jurisdiction, or not amenable to the process of the said Court
of Exchequer * in England or Ireland, or the Court of
Session in Scotland, or the courts of great sessions in
Wales, or shall be a bankrupt, insolvent, or lunatic,
or it shall be uncertain or unknown whether such
trustee is living or dead, that then and in such case
it shall and may be lawful to and for the judges of
the said courts respectively to order and direct that
the accountant general, or the secretary or deputy
secretary, or other proper officer for the time being of
the governor and company of the Bank of England,
do transfer in the books of the said company such
stock, annuities, or funds standing as aforesaid, to and
into the name of such person as such society may
appoint, and also pay over to such person as aforesaid the dividends of such stock, annuities, or funds;
and when and as often as it shall happen that one or
more only, and not all or both of such trustees as
aforesaid, shall be so absent, or not amenable to such
process as aforesaid, or a bankrupt, insolvent, or
lunatic, or it be uncertain or unknown whether any

Marginal note: When trus-tees shall be absent, &c., courts may order stock to be trans-ferred and dividends paid.

* Now the Court of Chancery.

one or more of such trustees is or are living or dead, that then, and in all and every such last-mentioned case and cases, it shall and may be lawful to and for the judges of the said courts respectively to order and direct that the other and others of such trustees who shall be forthcoming and ready and qualified to act do transfer such stock, annuities, or funds to and into the name of such person as aforesaid, and also that such forthcoming trustee do also receive and pay over the dividends of such stock, annuities, or funds, as such society shall direct; and that all such transfers and payments so made shall be and are hereby declared to be valid and effectual to all intents and purposes whatsoever, any former statute, law, usage, or custom to the contrary thereof in anywise notwithstanding.

No fee to be taken for any proceeding in such courts, &c.

XVII. And be it further enacted, That no fee, reward, emolument, or gratuity whatsoever shall be demanded, taken, or received by any officer or minister of such courts for any matter or thing done in such courts in pursuance of this Act; and that upon the presenting of any such petition it shall be lawful for the judges of the said courts respectively to assign counsel learned in the law, and to appoint a clerk or practitioner of such court, to advise and carry on such petition on the behalf of such society, who are hereby respectively required to do their duties therein without fee or reward.

Who shall be named in the orders of the court for making transfers.

XVIII. Provided always, and be it further enacted, That in all cases in which orders shall be made by any of the courts aforesaid for the transfer of stocks or funds transferable at the Bank of England the persons to be named in such orders respectively for making such transfers shall be the secretary, deputy secretary, or accountant general of the governor and company of the Bank of England for the time being, or one of them, except in cases where one or more of the trustees in whose name such stocks or funds shall stand shall be ordered to transfer the same without the concurrence of any other or others of such trustees, anything herein contained to the contrary thereof in anywise notwithstanding.

Act to be an indemnity to the bank.

XIX. And be it further enacted, That this Act shall be and is hereby declared to be a full and complete indemnity and discharge to the governor and company of the Bank of England, and their officers and servants, for all acts and things done or permitted to be done pursuant thereto, and that such acts and things shall not be questioned or impeached in any court of law or equity to their prejudice or detriment.

XX. [This section is repealed by 4 and 5 W. 4, c. 40, s. 12 *infra.*]

XXI. And be it further enacted, That all real and heritable property, monies, goods, chattels, and effects whatever, and all titles, securities for money, or other obligatory instruments and evidences or muniments, and all other effects whatever, and all rights or claims belonging to or had by such society, shall be vested in the treasurer or trustee of such society for the time being, for the use and benefit of such society and the respective members thereof, their respective executors or administrators, according to their respective claims and interests; and after the death or removal of any treasurer or trustee, shall vest in the succeeding treasurer or trustee, for the same estate and interest as the former treasurer or trustee had therein, and subject to the same trusts, without any assignment or conveyance whatever, except the transfer of stocks and securities in the public funds of Great Britain and Ireland, and also shall, for all purposes of action or suit, as well criminal as civil, in law or in equity, in anywise touching or concerning the same, be deemed and taken to be, and shall in every such proceeding (where necessary) be stated to be, the property of the person appointed to the office of treasurer or trustee of such society for the time being, in his or her proper name, without further description; and such person shall and he or she is hereby respectively authorized to bring or defend, or cause to be brought or defended, any action, suit, or prosecution, criminal as well as civil, in law or in equity, touching or concerning the property, right, or claim aforesaid of or belonging to or had by such society; provided such person shall have been thereunto duly authorized by the consent of the majority of members present at any meeting of the society or committee thereof; and such person so appointed shall and may, in all cases concerning the property, right, or claim aforesaid of such society, sue and be sued, plead and be impleaded, in his or her proper name, as treasurer or trustee of such society, without other description; and no such suit, action, or prosecution shall be discontinued or abate by the death of such person, or on his or her removal from the office of treasurer or trustee, but the same shall and may be proceeded in by the succeeding treasurer or trustee in the proper name of the person commencing the same, any law, usage, or custom to the contrary notwithstanding; and such succeeding treasurer or trustee shall pay or receive like costs as if the action or suit had been commenced in his or her name, for the benefit of or to be reimbursed from the funds of such society.

Limitation of responsibility of treasurers or trustees. XXII. And be it further enacted, That the treasurer or trustee, or any other officer of any society established under the authority of this Act, shall not be liable to make good any deficiency which may arise in the funds of such society, unless such persons shall have respectively declared by writing under their hands, deposited and registered in like manner with the rules of such society, that they are willing so to be answerable; and it shall be lawful for each of such persons, or for such persons collectively, to limit his, her, or their responsibility to such sum as shall be specified in any such instrument or writing : **Treasurer, &c. liable for money actually received.** Provided always, that the said treasurer, trustee, and every other the officer of any such society, shall be and they are hereby declared to be personally responsible and liable for all monies actually received by him, her, or them on account of or to and for the use of the said society.

Payment to persons appearing to be next of kin declared valid. XXIII. And be it further enacted, That whenever the trustees of any society established under this Act, at any time after the decease of any member, have paid and divided any sum of money to or amongst any person or persons who shall at the time of such payment appear to such trustees to be entitled to the effects of any deceased intestate member, the payment of any such sum or sums of money shall be valid and effectual with respect to any demand of any other person or persons as next of kin of such deceased intestate member, or as the lawful representative or representatives of such member, against the funds of such society or against the trustees thereof; but nevertheless such next of kin or representatives shall have remedy for such money so paid as aforesaid against the person or persons who shall have received the same.

For payment of sums not exceeding 20l. where members die intestate. XXIV. And be it further enacted, That in case any member of any society shall die, who shall be entitled to any sum not exceeding twenty pounds, it shall be lawful for the trustees or treasurer of such society, and they are hereby authorized and permitted, if such trustees or treasurer shall be satisfied that no will was made and left by such deceased member, and that no letters of administration or confirmation will be taken out, of the funds, goods, and chattels of such depositor, to pay the same at any time after the decease of such member according to the rules and regulations of the said institution; and in the event of there being no rules and regulations made in that behalf, then the said trustees or treasurer are hereby authorized and permitted to pay and divide the same to and amongst the person or persons entitled to the effects of the deceased intestate, and that without administration in England or Ireland, and without confirmation in Scotland.

XXV. And be it further enacted, That for the more effectually preventing fraud and imposition on the funds of such societies, if any officer, member, or any other person being or representing himself or herself to be a member of such society, or the nominee, executor, administrator, or assignee of any member of such society, or any other person whatever, shall in or by any false representation or imposition fraudulently obtain possession of the monies of such society or any part thereof, or, having in his or her possession any sum of money belonging to such society, shall fraudulently withhold the same, and for which offence no especial provision is made in the rules of such society, it shall be lawful for any one justice of the peace residing within the county within which such society shall be held, upon complaint made on oath or affirmation by an officer of such society appointed for that purpose, to summon such person against whom such complaint shall be made to appear at a time and place to be named in such summons; and upon his or her appearance, or, in default thereof, upon due proof, upon oath or affirmation of the service of such summons, it shall and may be lawful for any two justices residing within the county aforesaid to hear and determine the said complaint according to the rules of the said society, confirmed as directed by this Act; and upon due proof of such fraud the said justices shall convict the said party, and award double the amount of the money so fraudulently obtained or withheld to be paid to the treasurer, to be applied by him to the purposes of the society so proved to have been imposed upon and defrauded, together with such costs as shall be awarded by the said justices, not exceeding the sum of ten shillings; and in case such person against whom

[margin note: Justices may hear cases of fraud, and punish by fine or imprisonment.]

such complaint shall be made shall not pay the sum of money so awarded to the person and at the time specified in the said order, such justices are hereby required, by warrant under their hands and seals, to cause the same to be levied by distress and sale of the goods of such person on whom such order shall have been made or by other legal proceeding, together with such costs as shall be awarded by the said justices, not exceeding the sum of ten shillings, and also the costs and charges attending such distress and sale or other legal proceeding, returning the overplus (if any) to the owner; and, in default of such distress being found, the said justices of the peace shall commit such person so proved to have offended to the common gaol or house of correction, there to be kept to hard labour for such a period, not exceeding three calendar months, as to them shall seem fit : Provided nevertheless, that nothing herein contained shall prevent the said society from proceeding by indictment or complaint against the party complained of ; and provided also, that no party shall be proceeded against by indictment or complaint, if a previous conviction has been obtained for the same offence under the provisions of this Act.

Proceedings necessary for the dissolution of any society.

XXVI. And be it further enacted, That it shall not be lawful for any such society, by any rule at any general meeting, or otherwise, to dissolve or determine such society, so long as the intents or purposes declared by such society, or any of them, remain to be carried into effect, without obtaining the votes of consent of five-sixths in value of the then existing members of such society, to be ascertained in manner hereinafter mentioned, and also the consent of all persons then receiving or then entitled to receive relief from such society, either on account of sickness, age, or infirmity, to be testified under their hands individually and respectively ; and for the purpose of ascertaining the votes of such five-sixths in value, every member shall be entitled to one vote, and an additional vote for every five years that he may have been a member : Provided also, that no one member shall have more than five votes in the whole ; and in all cases of dissolution, the intended appropriation or division of the funds or other property of such society shall be fairly and distinctly stated in the proposed

Stock not divisible but for general purposes of the society.

plan of dissolution, prior to such consent being given; nor shall it be lawful for such society by any rule to direct the division or distribution of such stock or fund, or any part thereof, to or amongst the several members of such society, other than for carrying into effect the general intents and purposes of such society, declared by them, and confirmed by the justices of the peace as aforesaid, according to the directions of this Act, but that all such rules for the dissolution or determination of any such society, without such consent as aforesaid, or for the distribution or division of the stock or fund of such society, contrary to the rules which shall have been confirmed by the said justices at their sessions, and filed in pursuance of this Act, shall be void and of none effect; and in the event of such division or misappropriation of the funds of such society, without the consent hereby declared to be requisite, the trustee or other officer or person aiding or abetting therein shall be liable to the like penalties as are hereinbefore provided for in cases of fraud.*

Penalties for illegal dissolution or division of funds.

XXVII. Provided always, and be it further enacted, That provision shall be made by one or more of the rules of every such society, to be confirmed as required by this Act, specifying whether a reference of every matter in dispute between any such society or any person acting under them, and any individual member thereof, or person claiming on account of any member, shall be made to such of His Majesty's justices of the peace as may act in and for the county in which such society may be formed, or to arbitrators to be appointed in manner hereinafter directed; and if the matter so in dispute shall be referred to arbitration, certain arbitrators shall be named and elected at the first meeting of such society, or general committee thereof, that shall be held after the enrolment of its rules, none of the said arbitrators being beneficially interested, directly or indirectly, in the funds of the said society, of whom a certain number, not less than three, shall be chosen by ballot in each such case of dispute, the number of the said arbitrators and mode of ballot being determined by the rules of each society respectively; the names of such arbitrators shall be duly entered in the book of the said society in which the rules are entered as aforesaid; and in case of the death, or refusal, or neglect of any or all of the said arbitrators to act, it shall and may be lawful to and for the said society, or general

Rules to be made directing how disputes shall be settled.

Appointment of arbitrators.

---

* The first part of this section, as to the dissolution of a society, does not apply to Benefit Building Societies.

committee thereof, and they are hereby required, at
their next meeting, to name and elect one or more
arbitrator or arbitrators as aforesaid to act in the
place of the said arbitrator or arbitrators so dying, or
refusing or neglecting to act as aforesaid ; and whatever award shall be made by the said arbitrators, or
the major part of them, according to the true purport
and meaning of the rules of such society, confirmed
by the justices according to the directions of this Act,
shall be in the form to this Act annexed, and shall
be binding and conclusive on all parties, and shall be
final, to all intents and purposes, without appeal, or
being subject to the control of one or more justices
of the peace, and shall not be removed or removable
into any court of law, or restrained or restrainable by

Justices shall enforce compliance with the decision of arbitrators. the injunction of any court of equity ; and should either
of the said parties in dispute refuse or neglect to
comply with or conform to the decision of the said
arbitrators or the major part of them, it shall and
may be lawful for any one justice of the peace residing within the county within which such society
shall be held, upon good and sufficient proof being
adduced before him of such award having been made,
and of the refusal of the party to comply therewith,
upon complaint made by or on behalf of the party
aggrieved, to summon the person against whom such
complaint shall be made to appear at a time and place
to be named in such summons ; and upon his or her
appearance, or in default thereof, upon due proof,
upon oath, of the service of such summons, any two
justices of the peace may proceed to make such order
thereupon as to them may seem just ; and if the sum
of money so awarded, together with a sum for costs
not exceeding the sum of ten shillings, as to such
justices shall seem meet, shall not be immediately
paid, then such justices shall, by warrant under their
hands and seals, cause such sum and costs as aforesaid to be levied by distress or by distress and sale
of the monies, goods, chattels, securities, and effects
belonging to the said party or to the said society, or
other legal proceeding, together with all further costs
and charges attending such distress and sale or other
legal proceeding, returning the overplus (if any) to
the said party, or to the said society, or to one of the
treasurers or trustees thereof ; and in default of such
distress being found, or such other legal proceeding
being ineffectual, then to be levied by distress and
sale of the proper goods of the said party or of the

officer of the said society so neglecting or refusing as aforesaid, by other legal proceedings, together with such further costs and charges as aforesaid, returning the overplus (if any) to the owner : Provided always, that whatever sums shall be paid by any such officer, so levied on his or her property or goods in pursuance of the award of arbitrators or order of any justices, shall be repaid, with all damages accruing to him or her, by and out of the monies belonging to such society, or out of the first monies which shall be thereafter received by such society.

XXVIII. And be it further enacted, That if by the rules of any such society it is directed that any matter in dispute as aforesaid shall be decided by justices of the peace, it shall and may be lawful for any such justice, on complaint being made to him of any refusal or neglect to comply with the rules of such society by any member or officer thereof, to summon the person against whom such complaint shall be made to appear at a time and place to be named in such summons ; and upon his or her appearance, or in default thereof, upon due proof, on oath or affirmation, of the service of such summons, it shall and may be lawful for any two justices to proceed to hear and determine the said complaint according to the rules of the said society; and in case the said justices shall adjudge any sum of money to be paid by such person against whom such complaint shall be made, and such person shall not pay such sum of money to the person and at the time specified by such justices, they shall proceed to enforce their award in the manner hereinbefore directed to be used in case of any neglect to comply with the decision of the arbitrators appointed under the authority of this Act. *Reference of disputes to justices, if so directed by the rules of the society.*

XXIX. And be it further enacted, That every sentence, order, and adjudication of any justices under this Act shall be final and conclusive to all intents and purposes, and shall not be subject to appeal, and shall not be removed or removable into any court of law, or restrained or restrainable by the injunction of any court of equity, and that no suspension, advocation, or reduction shall be competent. *Orders of justices to be final.*

XXX., XXXI. [These sections authorize friendly societies to invest their funds in savings banks or with the National Debt Commissioners.]

XXXII. [This section allows minors to be members.]

Societies shall make annual audits and statements of the funds to the members.

XXXIII. And be it further enacted, That the rules of every such society shall provide that the treasurers, trustees, stewards, or other principal officer thereof shall, once in every year at least, prepare or cause to be prepared a general statement of the funds and effects of or belonging to such society, specifying in whose custody or possession the said funds or effects shall be then remaining, together with an account of all and every the various sums of money received and expended by or on account of the said society since the publication of the preceding periodical statement, and every such periodical statement shall be attested by two or more members of such society appointed anditors for that purpose, and shall be countersigned by the secretary or clerk of such society; and every member shall be entitled to receive from the said society a copy of such periodical statement, on payment of such sum as the rules of such society may require, not exceeding the sum of sixpence.

XXXIV., XXXV., XXXVI. [These sections relate to the making of returns of sickness and mortality.]

Exemption from stamp duties.

XXXVII. And be it further enacted, that no copy of rules, power, warrant, or letter of attorney granted or to be granted by any person as trustees of any society established under this Act, for the transfer of any share in the public funds standing in the name of such trustee, nor any receipts given for any dividend in any public stock or fund or interest of exchequer bills, nor any receipt, nor any entry in any book of receipt, for money deposited in the funds of any such society, nor for any money received by any member, his or her executors or administrators, assigns or attornies, from the funds of such society, nor any bond nor other security to be given to or on account of any such society, or by the treasurer or trustee or any officer thereof, nor any draft or order, nor any form of assurance, nor any appointment of any agent, nor any certificate or other instrument for the revocation of any such appointment, nor any other instrument or document whatever required or authorized to be given, issued, signed, made, or produced in pursuance of this Act, shall be subject or liable to or charged with any stamp duty or duties whatsoever.

Construction of Act.

XXXVIII. And be it further enacted, That the word "Society" in this Act shall be understood to include Friendly Society or Societies, Institution or Institutions; the word "Rules" to include Rules, Orders, and Regulations; the word "County" to

include County, Riding, Division, or Place; and the
words "Treasurer or Trustee" to include Treasurers
or Trustees; and the word "Person" to include
Persons; and the word "Book" to include Books;
and the word "Bond" to include Bonds; "Name"
to include Names; "Account" to include Accounts;
"Member" to include Members and Honorary Members; "Clerk of the Peace" to include Town Clerk;
unless it be otherwise specially provided.

XXXIX., XL. [These sections relate to friendly
societies already enrolled.]

XLI. And be it further enacted, That this Act Public Act.
shall be deemed a public Act, and shall extend to
Great Britain and Ireland and Berwick-upon-Tweed,
and be judicially taken notice of as such by all
judges, justices, and other persons whatsoever, without the same being specially shown or pleaded.

SCHEDULE.

FORM OF AWARD.

We, the major part of the arbitrators duly appointed by
the   Society established at   in the
county of   do hereby award and order, That
A. B. [*specifying by name the party or the officer of the Society*]
do, on the   day of   , pay to *C. D.*
the sum of   [*or* we do hereby reinstate in
or expel *A. B.* from the said Society, *as the case may be*].
Dated this   day of   one thousand eight
hundred and

                                                            E. F.
                                                            G. H.

FORM OF BOND.

Know all Men by these Presents, That we, *A. B.* of
                    treasurer [*or* trustee, &c.] of the
Society established at   in the county of
                    , and *C. D.* of   and *G. H.* of
                    (as sureties on behalf of the said *A. B.*), are
jointly and severally held and firmly bound to *E. F.*, the
present Clerk of the Peace [*or* Town Clerk] for the county [*or*
county of a city, *or* county of a town, riding, division, *or*
place, *as the case may be*] of   in the sum of

to be paid to the said *E. F.* as such Clerk of the Peace [*or* Town Clerk] or his successor, Clerk of the Peace [*or* Town Clerk] of the said county [*or* county of a city, &c.] for the time being, or his certain attorney; for which payment well and truly to be made we jointly and severally bind ourselves, and each of us by himself, our and each of our heirs, executors, and administrators, firmly by these presents, sealed with our seals. Dated the   day of   in the   year of our Lord

Whereas the above-bounden *A. B.* hath been duly appointed treasurer [*or* trustee, &c.] of the   Society established as aforesaid, and he, together with the above-bounden *C. D.* and *G. H.* as his sureties, have entered into the above-written Bond, subject to the condition hereinafter contained; now, therefore, the condition of the above-written Bond is such, that if the said *A. B.* shall and do justly and faithfully execute his office of treasurer [*or* trustee] of the said Society established as aforesaid, and shall and do render a just and true account of all monies received and paid by him, and shall and do pay over all the monies remaining in his hands, and assign and transfer or deliver all securities and effects, books, papers, and property of or belonging to the said Society in his hands or custody to such person or persons as the said Society shall appoint, according to the rules of the said Society, together with the proper or legal receipts or vouchers for such payments, and likewise shall and do in all respects well and truly and faithfully perform and fulfil his office of treasurer [*or* trustee, &c.] to the said Society, according to the rules thereof, then the above-written Bond shall be void and of no effect, otherwise it shall be and remain in full force and virtue.

---

4 & 5 WILL. 4, CAP. 40.

An Act to amend an Act of the Tenth Year of His late Majesty King George the Fourth, to consolidate and amend the Laws relating to Friendly Societies.
[*30th July* 1834.]

10 G. 4, c. 56.   Whereas it is expedient to alter and amend an Act made in the tenth year of the reign of his late Majesty King George the Fourth, intituled An Act to consolidate and amend the Laws relating to Friendly Societies : Be it therefore enacted by the King's most

excellent Majesty, by and with the advice and consent of the lords spiritual and temporal, and commons, in this present parliament assembled, and by the authority of the same, that so much of the said Act as enacts that no rules shall be allowed unless it shall appear to the justices to whom the same are tendered that the tables of the payment to be made by the members, and of the benefits to be received by them, may be adopted with safety to all parties concerned ; and so much as enacts that the executors, administrators, or assignees of bankrupts or insolvents shall pay money due to friendly societies before any other debts ; and so much as enacts that the funds of any friendly society may be subscribed into a savings bank ; and so much as requires the returns of the rate of sickness and mortality to be made to the clerk of the peace, or as requires clerks of the peace to transmit such returns to the Secretary of State, or as provides that the Friendly Society refusing or neglecting to make such return should cease to be entitled to the privileges of the said recited Act ; shall be and the same are hereby repealed.

Repeal of 10 G. 4, c. 56, s. 6.

s. 20.

s. 30.

Part of s. 34.

Part of s. 35.

s. 36.

III. And be it further enacted, That so much of the said recited Act as relates to the rules of Friendly Societies being transmitted to the barrister or advocate, and deposited with the clerk of the peace and certified by him, as well as so much as relates to alterations of rules being certified by the clerk of the peace, and that no rule or alteration or amendment should be binding until confirmed by the justices, and filed under the recited Act, shall be and the same are hereby repealed.

Repeal of 10 G. 4, c. 56, s. 4, and part of s. 7.

IV. And be it further enacted, that two transcripts, fairly written on paper or parchment, of all rules made in pursuance of the said recited Act or this Act, signed by three members, and countersigned by the clerk or secretary (accompanied, in the case of an alteration or amendment of rules, with an affidavit of the clerk or secretary or one of the officers of the said society that the provisions of the said recited Act, or of the Act under which the rules of the society may have been enrolled, have been duly complied with), with all convenient speed after the same shall be made, altered, or amended, and so from time to time, after every making, altering, or amending thereof, shall be submitted, in England and Wales and Berwick-upon-Tweed, to the barrister-at-law for the time being appointed to certify the rules of savings

Two transcripts of rules to be submitted to a barrister &c., by whom they are to be certified.

D

banks, and in Scotland to the lord advocate or any depute appointed by him for that purpose, and in Ireland to such barrister as may be appointed by His Majesty's attorney-general in Ireland, for the purpose of ascertaining whether the said rules of such society, or alteration or amendment thereof, are calculated to carry into effect the intention of the parties framing such rules, alterations, or amendments, and are in conformity to law and to the provisions of the said

recited Act or this Act; and that the said barrister or advocate shall advise with the said clerk or secretary, if required, and shall give a certificate on each of the said transcripts, that the same are in conformity to law and to the provisions of the said recited Act and this Act, or point out in what part or parts the said rules are repugnant thereto; and that the bar-

rister or advocate, for advising as aforesaid, and perusing the rules, or alterations or amendments of the rules, of each respective society, and giving such certificates as aforesaid, shall demand no further fee

than that specified in the said recited Act; and one of such transcripts, when certified by the said barrister or advocate, shall be returned to the society, and the other of such transcripts shall be transmitted by such barrister or advocate to the clerk of the peace for the county wherein such society shall be formed, and by him laid before the justices for such county at the general quarter sessions, or adjournment thereof, held next after the time when such transcript shall have been so certified and transmitted to him as

aforesaid; and the justices then and there present are hereby authorised and required, without motion, to allow and confirm the same; and such transcript

shall be filed by such clerk of the peace with the rolls of the sessions of the peace in his custody, with-

out fee or reward; and that all rules, alterations, and amendments thereof, from the time when the same shall be certified by the said barrister or advocate, shall be binding on the several members and officers of the said society, and all other persons having interest therein.

V. Provided always, and be it enacted, that the said barrister shall be entitled to no further fee for or in respect of any alteration or amendment of any rules upon which one fee has been already paid to the said barrister within the period of three years: provided also, that if any rules, alterations or amendments, are sent to such barrister or advocate, accompanied with an affidavit of being a copy of any rules, or alterations or amendments of the rules, of any other society, which shall have been already enrolled under the provisions of the said recited Act or this Act, the said barrister or advocate shall certify and return the same as aforesaid, without being entitled to any fee for such certificate.

being copies of those already enrolled.

VI. [This section relates to the returns of sickness.]

VII. And whereas in and by the said recited Act provision is directed to be made by the rules of every society whether reference of any matter in dispute shall be made to justices or to arbitrators : and whereas it is expedient that further provision should be made in case the reference is to arbitrators : Be it therefore enacted, that when the rules of any society provide for a reference to arbitrators of any matter in dispute, and it shall appear to any justice of the peace, on the complaint on oath of a member of any such society, or of any person claiming on account of such member, that application has been made to such society, or the steward or other officer thereof, for the purpose of having any dispute so settled by arbitration, and that such application has not within forty days been complied with, or that the arbitrators have neglected or refused to make any award, it shall and may be lawful for such justice to summon the trustee, treasurer, steward, or other officer of the society, or any one of them against whom the complaint is made, and for any two justices to hear and determine the matter in dispute, in the same manner as if the rules of the said society had directed that any matter in dispute as aforesaid should be decided by justices of the peace, anything in the said recited Act contained to the contrary notwithstanding.

If rules of society direct reference in case of dispute to arbitration, and society refuse to grant arbitrators, &c., justices may determine the dispute.

VIII. And be it further enacted, that in case any member of a Friendly Society established under the said recited Act or this Act shall have been expelled from such society, and the arbitrators or justices, as the case may be, shall award or order that he or she shall be reinstated, it shall and may be lawful for such arbitrators or justices to award or order, in default of such reinstatement, to the member so expelled, such a sum of money as to such arbitrators or justices may seem just and reasonable ; which said sum of money, if not paid, shall be recoverable from the said society, or the treasurer, trustee, or other officer, in the same way as any money awarded by arbitrators is recoverable under the said recited Act.

Provision in case member of society is expelled.

IX. [This section relates to investment of funds in Savings Banks, and is repealed by section 6 of the Benefit Building Societies Act.]

Members of friendly societies may be witnesses.

X. And be it further enacted, That on the trial of any action, indictment, or other proceeding respecting the property of any society enrolled under the authority of the said recited Act or this Act, or in any proceedings before any justice of the peace, any member of such society shall be a competent witness, and shall not be objected to on account of any interests he may have as such member in the result of such action, indictment, or other proceeding.

XI. [No fee to be taken for oath taken in reference to sick pay.]

Executors, &c., of officers of friendly society to pay money due to society before any other debts.

XII. And be it further enacted, That if any person already appointed, or who may hereafter be appointed to any office in a society established under the said recited Act or this Act, and being entrusted with the keeping of the accounts, or having in his hands or possession, by virtue of his said office or employment, any moneys or effects belonging to such society, or any deeds or securities relating to the same, shall die, or become a bankrupt or insolvent, or have any execution, or attachment or other process issued, or action or diligence raised, against his lands, goods, chattels, or effects, or property or estate, heritable or movable, or make any assignment, disposition, assignation, or other conveyance thereof for the benefit of his creditors, his heirs, executors, administrators, or assignees, or other persons having legal right, or the sheriff or other officer executing such process, or the party using such action or diligence, shall, within forty days after demand made in writing by the order of any such society or committee thereof, or the major part of them assembled at any meeting thereof, deliver and pay over all moneys and other things belonging to such society to such person as such society or committee shall appoint, and shall pay, out of the estates, assets, or effects, heritable or movable, of such person, all sums of money remaining due which such person received by virtue of his said office or employment, before any other of his debts are paid or satisfied, or before the money directed to be levied by such process as aforesaid, or which may be recovered or recoverable under such diligence, is paid over to the party issuing such process or using such diligence and all such assets, lands, goods, chattels, property estates, and effects shall be bound to the payment and discharge thereof accordingly.

XIII.—XIV. [These sections relate to the postage of letters and former Friendly Societies.]

XV. And be it further enacted, That wherever in the said recited Act or this Act, in describing or referring to any person, the word importing the singular number or the masculine gender only is used, the same shall be understood to include and shall be applied to several persons or parties as well as one person or party, and females as well as males, unless there be something in the subject or context repugnant to such construction. *Construction of words in the Act.*

XVI. And be it further enacted, That this Act may be altered, amended, or repealed during the present session of parliament. *Act may be amended.*

XVII. And be it further enacted, that this Act shall be deemed a public Act, and shall extend to Great Britain and Ireland and Berwick-upon-Tweed, and be judicially taken notice of as such by all judges, justices, and other persons whatsoever, without the same being specially shown or pleaded. *Public Act.*

APPENDIX.

RULES FOR A PERMANENT BENEFIT BUILDING SOCIETY.

NAME AND OBJECT.

THIS Society shall be called the   Benefit Building Society, and is established for the purpose of raising by Monthly Subscriptions of   per Share, not exceeding   each, a stock or fund to enable each or any Member to receive out of the funds of the Society, the amount or value of his Share or Shares therein, to erect or purchase one or more dwelling-house or dwelling-houses, or other real or leasehold estate, to be secured by way of mortgage to the Society until the amount or value of his Share or Shares shall have been repaid to the Society, with all fines and other payments incurred in respect thereof.

ENTRANCE FEE.

The Entrance Fee shall be 2s. 6d. per Share, and so in proportion for any part of a Share.

CERTIFICATE OF SHARES.

Every Member, upon subscribing for a Share or Shares, and signing the Share Register Book in respect thereof as hereinafter provided, shall be entitled to a certificate or certificates of such Share or Shares, specifying the numbers and amount thereof, respectively signed by three Directors and countersigned by the Secretary, which certificate shall be evidence of his title thereto.

In case a certificate of Shares shall be lost, the owner shall be entitled to a duplicate thereof, upon making a statutory declaration of the loss of the original, and of his title thereto, and upon paying a fine of 5s. per Share.

AMOUNT OF SHARES AND SUBSCRIPTION.

The Shares shall be of the ultimate value of   each.
The Subscription for each Share shall be   per month for the
full term of   years, to commence from the
day of the month the Member shall be admitted in respect of
each Share ; and such Subscription shall be payable in advance
at the first monthly Subscription Meeting of the Society after
the admittance of the Member.

Any Member holding one or more Shares may, with the
consent of the Board of Directors, subscribe for a part of
another Share.

MONTHLY SUBSCRIPTION MEETINGS.

The monthly Subscription Meetings of the Society shall
be held at
or at such other place in the said County   as
the Board of Directors shall from time to time appoint on
the first   in every month, from   o'clock until
o'clock in the evening, or at such other days and hours as the
Board of Directors shall from time to time direct, and of which
one week's notice, signed by the Secretary, shall have been
given to the Members.

ANNUAL AND HALF-YEARLY MEETINGS.

The Annual Meeting of the Society shall be held on the
            day in the month of   in every year,
and the Half-Yearly Meeting on
between the hours of   o'clock and   o'clock in
the evening, at the same place where the last Monthly Subscription Meeting shall have been held, or at such other time
or place in the said County or City as the Board of Directors
shall from time to time appoint, and of which one week's
notice, signed by the Secretary, shall have been given to the
Members.

At every Annual Meeting of the Society a general Report,
signed by three Directors and the Secretary, showing the
transactions of the Society during the past year, its present
condition and the state of its affairs generally, and the Auditors'
Report and Balance-sheet shall be read to the Society, and the
books and accounts, and the statement of accounts, audited
and approved by the Auditors, shall be produced for the
inspection of the Members ; new Directors and Auditors shall
be elected in the place of those who shall retire from office, and
other vacant offices (if any) filled up ; and the present state and

future prospects of the Society may be discussed, and such other business transacted as may be deemed proper and expedient.

MANAGEMENT.

The business and affairs of the Society shall be managed and conducted by a Board of Directors.

DIRECTORS.

There shall be twelve Directors of the Society ; and

shall be the first and present Directors of the Society.

Every Director shall be a subscriber for   Shares at least in the Society.

The Directors shall meet together on the in every month during the continuance of the Society, or oftener if necessary, at such place in the said County and at such hour as they shall think fit, for the purpose of conducting the business of the Society, and every such meeting at which not less than three Directors are present, shall be styled a Board of Directors.

At the first meeting of the Directors after their election, the Directors present shall elect one of their body as Chairman ; and in the event of his absence at any of the subsequent meetings of the Board, a Chairman for the evening shall be appointed by the Directors present.

No business shall be entered upon or transacted at any such meeting, unless three Directors at least are present, and every question shall be decided by a majority of votes.

Every Director present, including the Chairman, shall have one vote ; and in case the votes are equal, the Chairman shall have a casting vote.

Minutes of all the proceedings of every Board of Directors shall be entered in a book to be kept for that purpose, and the minutes so entered shall be signed in the book at the next meeting of the Board, either by the person who was in the chair, or by a Director not in the chair who was present at that meeting.

At every meeting of the Board of Directors, immediately after the minutes of the last meeting shall have been read and signed, the Bankers' book shall be produced and inspected, and the amounts received on account of the Society since the last meeting shall be declared ; and the total amount thereof, with the amount of the balance remaining in the hands of the Bankers, shall be entered in the Minute Book ; after which applications for withdrawals and advances shall be recorded and considered.

The Board of Directors shall also from time to time inspect the books and accounts kept by the Secretary, and shall have power to appoint agents to transact any business for the Society, and to pay them out of the funds of the Society such remuneration for their services as they shall think reasonable.

Four Directors shall go out of office in rotation every year at the Annual Meeting, and four others shall be elected in their place by show of hands, or by ballot, if demanded by any Member ; but the Directors so retiring shall be eligible to be re-elected.

Any two of the Directors may call a Special Meeting of the Board, by giving at least two clear days' notice.

If any Director shall die, or be desirous of resigning, or shall become incapable to act as Director, or shall become bankrupt or insolvent, or compound with his creditors, or shall borrow the amount or value of his Shares out of the funds of the Society, or shall be removed from his office by a resolution of a Special General Meeting of the Members, he shall thereupon cease to be a Director of the Society ; and the Secretary shall forthwith convene a Special Meeting of the Board of Directors, and at such Special Meeting the Board shall appoint another Member of the Society to be a Director in his place.

TRUSTEES.

There shall be   Trustees of the Society, and

shall be the first and present Trustees, and shall continue in office during the pleasure of the Members.

The Trustees shall be admitted to all meetings of the Board of Directors, and shall be at liberty to take part in the proceedings thereof, but shall not vote on any question under discussion unless they are qualified in like manner as the Directors.

All the moneys and funds of the Society shall be paid into the hands of the Bankers to the credit of the Trustees of the Society.

All Deeds and Securities shall be taken in the names of the Trustees for the time being, and shall be deposited in a fire-proof chest, or fire-proof room, to which there shall be three keys, one of which shall be kept by a Trustee, another by the Chairman of the Board of Directors, and the third by the Solicitor or Solicitors for the time being to the said Society, and the chest shall be placed for safe custody with the Bankers of the Society, in the names of the Trustees, and a Schedule of the deeds therein from time to time shall be deposited in the box, and a copy thereof shall be kept in a book by the Secretary.

All advances and payments out of the funds of the Society shall be made by cheques on the Bankers of the Society, signed at a Board of Directors by one Trustee, and at least two Directors, or in case there shall be no Trustee present at the Board, then by three Directors, the Chairman being one; and every cheque shall be countersigned by the Secretary.

All proceedings at law or in equity which it shall be necessary to prosecute or defend on behalf of the Society, in the names of the Trustees of the Society, shall be brought or defended by the Solicitor of the Society; and the Trustees of the Society shall be indemnified and saved harmless out of the funds of the Society from all loss in respect thereof.

In case either of the Trustees shall be desirous to be discharged from, or shall become incapacitated to act in the trusts reposed in him, or shall become bankrupt or insolvent, or compound with his creditors, or shall borrow the amount or value of all or any of his Shares out of the funds of the Society, he shall be removed from his office by the resolution of a Special General Meeting of the Members, and shall thereupon cease to be a Trustee of the Society, and the Secretary shall forthwith convene a Special Meeting of the Board of Directors; and at such Special Meeting a new Trustee shall be elected in the place of such Trustee, or of a Trustee dying; and the appointment of every new Trustee shall be signed by one of the continuing Trustees (if any such there be) and three Directors, and be duly certified as a rule of the Society; and thereupon all the property of the Society vested in such retiring Trustee, either alone or jointly with the continuing Trustees or Trustee, shall vest in the new Trustee appointed in his place for the same estate and interest as the former Trustee had therein, and subject to the same trusts, without any assignment or conveyance whatsoever, except the transfer of stocks and securities in the Government Stocks or Funds of Great Britain and Ireland (if any), and all such stocks and securities, and all other property and effects (if any) which cannot be legally and effectually vested in the new and continuing Trustees or Trustee, without any conveyance, assignment, or transfer, by virtue of these Rules and the provisions of the 10 Geo. 4, cap. 56, section 21, and the 6 & 7 Will. 4, cap. 32, section 4, shall be conveyed, assigned, and transferred at the expense of the Society, so as to vest in such new and continuing Trustees or Trustee upon the trusts, and with the powers under and subject to which the same ought to be held by the Trustees of the Society.

That in the meantime, and until the appointment of such new Trustee, the continuing Trustees shall be competent to act as fully as if they were the sole Trustees of the Society.

The Trustees respectively shall be chargeable only for their own acts and defaults respectively, and not for the acts or defaults of the others or other of them, nor for the acts or defaults of any other person or persons.

In case any Trustee, or the heirs, executors, or administrators of any Trustee so dying, or being removed as aforesaid, shall neglect or refuse to convey, assign, or transfer to the new and continuing Trustees, and as the Board of Directors shall direct, any property or effects of the Society which may be vested in him, either alone or jointly, with the continuing Trustees or Trustee, within seven days after he shall have been required so to do in writing under the hand of the Secretary and two Directors, pursuant to a resolution of the Board of Directors, the Trustee or other person or persons so neglecting or refusing shall be expelled the Society, and shall forfeit all moneys paid by him or them to the Society, and shall wholly cease to have any estate or interest therein; and the amount or value of his or their Share or Shares in the Society shall be transferred to the credit of the contingent fund of the Society, for the benefit of the other Members interested therein, and he or they shall be compelled by all legal and equitable means to make and execute such conveyance, assignment, or transfer, as may have been required of him or them as aforesaid.

SECRETARY.

Mr.   shall be the first and present Secretary of the Society.

The Secretary shall attend every meeting of the Directors or Members of the Society, and shall enter in a rough Minute Book true and correct minutes of all the proceedings of every such meeting, and of all the resolutions passed, and the business transacted thereat, and such minutes he shall afterwards fairly copy in another book, to be read at the next meeting of the like nature, and signed by the Chairman.

He shall also keep all the other books and the accounts of the Society, convene all Special Meetings of the Directors and of the Members, issue all notices, conduct the correspondence of the Society, under the direction of the Board of Directors, and transact such other business as the Board shall from time to time direct.

In the month of   in every year he shall prepare from the books of the Society a correct statement of accounts and balance-sheet for the Auditors ; and in the month of
in every year he shall prepare a Report of the past year's transactions, showing the present condition of the Society, and the state of its affairs, to be submitted to the Board of Directors for approval, and approved by them previously to its being printed and circulated amongst the Members.

The Secretary shall have the custody of all the books, papers, and accounts of the Society (except deeds and securities for money), and at every monthly Subscription Meeting he shall produce the books and accounts of the Society for the inspection of such of the Members as may wish to inspect them, and he shall at all times, whenever required so to do, produce to any Director or Trustee, or to such person or persons as any Director or Trustee may direct, in writing, any book, paper, or account belonging to the Society or relating to the business or affairs thereof, and shall permit copies to be made thereof, or of any part thereof, or extracts to be taken therefrom, and shall give to any Director or Trustee such information as he may from time to time require concerning the Society or its business or affairs.

At every monthly Subscription Meeting the Secretary shall receive from the Members the Subscriptions and all Fines and other payments due to the Society, and at the time of the receipt thereof he shall enter the same in the Cash Book, with the name of the Member paying the same, and at the close of the meeting he shall account for and pay over to the Treasurer the total amount of such receipts, and procure the Treasurer's signature to an acknowledgment of such payment in the Cash Book.

The Secretary shall be allowed out of the funds of the Society for his services a salary of £   per annum, and a fee of
per annum on every Share subscribed for; such salary and allowance to be paid quarterly.

SOLICITORS.

Messrs.   shall be the first and present Solicitors of the Society.

The Solicitors shall carefully investigate the title to every property that shall be offered as a security to the Society, after the same shall have been reported by the Surveyor as of adequate value, and approved by the Board of Directors, and when necessary consult counsel thereon, and shall report in writing the result of such investigation to the Board of Directors.

They shall prepare all the Mortgage Securities and such

other Deeds, Conveyances, and writings as may be necessary for the purposes of the Society, and they shall be held responsible for the due and proper execution of such deeds, and the deposit thereof, and of the Title Deeds and writings relating thereto, before any advance is made out of the funds of the Society upon the security thereof; and upon the completion of every mortgage security and the deposit thereof, and of the Title Deeds and writings relating thereto in their hands, they shall deliver to the Mortgagor, or to such person as he shall direct, a cheque or cheques upon the Bankers of the Society for the amount of the advance to which such Mortgagor shall be entitled, duly signed as required by these Rules, and shall obtain upon the back of every such cheque the signature of such Mortgagor; and within seven days after the completion of every Mortgage the Solicitor shall deposit the mortgage, and all deeds and writings relating thereto, in the deed-box of the Society, to be kept at the Bankers, as provided by these Rules, with a list or schedule of such deeds and writings, and shall deliver a copy of such list or schedule to the Secretary of the Society; and within ten days after the completion of every Mortgage the Solicitor shall insure such part or parts of the property comprised in the Mortgage as shall be insurable from loss or damage by fire, in such office as the Board of Directors shall from time to time appoint, and shall transact all other legal business of the Society.

The Solicitor shall be entitled to attend all meetings of the Board of Directors and all the meetings of the Members; but he shall not be entitled to vote on any question unless he be a Shareholder.

The Solicitor's charges shall be paid by the Member on whose account they may be incurred, either out of the advance to which such Member shall be entitled, or, if no advance shall be made, then out of the proper moneys of such Member, who shall pay the amount at the next monthly Subscription Meeting; and in default of payment such Member shall be fined as for an equal amount of subscriptions in arrear.

Should any Member object to the amount of the Solicitor's Bill of Costs against him, or any charges therein, such bill shall, if the amount be not otherwise settled, be taxed by the proper officer, as between attorney and client, in the usual manner.

SURVEYORS.

Messrs.   shall be the first and present Surveyors of the Society.

The Surveyors shall attend all meetings of the Board of Directors, and on receiving instructions in writing from the

Secretary they shall, within seven days from the date thereof, survey any property offered as security to the Society, and furnish the Board of Directors at their next monthly meeting with a map or ground plan thereof, and a report in writing stating the rent and value of the property, and such other particulars concerning the same as shall from time to time be required by the Board of Directors.

He shall be paid for his survey by the member whose property shall be surveyed, or out of the advance, if any, which shall be made to him as follows—that is to say, if the advance required be the value of one Share,   Shillings; two Shares,   Shillings; three Shares,   Shillings; and for every additional Share above three,   ; but if the property be more than three miles distant from his place of residence, he shall be paid by such Member such a sum not exceeding   per mile in addition to the above charges, as the Board of Directors shall from time to time determine to be fair and reasonable, and he shall also be paid by such Member for the Map or Ground Plan of the Premises, such a sum not exceeding   as the Board of Directors shall in each case think fair and reasonable. If no advance shall be made to the Member whose property shall have been surveyed, the Surveyor's charges shall be paid at the next monthly Subscription Meeting, and in default of payment such Member shall be fined as for an equal amount of subscription in arrear.

TREASURER.

Mr.   of   , shall be the first and present Treasurer of the Society.

The Treasurer shall attend every monthly Subscription Meeting of the Society, and at the close thereof shall examine and check the Secretary's account of Subscriptions, Fines, and other Money paid at such Meeting, and at the close of the Meeting he shall receive from the Secretary the total amount of his receipts, and sign an acknowledgment thereof in the Cash Book, and on the following day he shall pay the amount into the hands of the Society's Bankers, to the credit of the Trustees of the Society.

The current expenses, and all payments on account of the Society (except advances made to the Members, for which cheques shall in all cases be delivered to the Member entitled to receive the same) shall be paid by the Treasurer, who shall, from time to time, obtain from one of the Trustees and two of the Directors a cheque for the necessary amount, countersigned by the Secretary; and the Treasurer shall, at the next monthly Subscription Meeting, deliver to the Secretary proper vouchers for such payments respectively, and the Secretary shall enter such payments respectively in the proper book, and sign an acknowledgment thereof in the Treasurer's Cash Book.

BANKERS.

Messrs.   shall be the first and present Bankers of the Society.

All moneys of or belonging to the Society shall be paid into the hands of the Bankers to the credit of the Trustees of the Society, for the time being, and no payment shall be made thereout by the Bankers, except upon a cheque signed by one Trustee and two of the Directors for the time being, or by three Directors, and countersigned by the Secretary for the time being.

The Bankers shall keep the Deed-box of the Society, and shall not permit the same to be removed out of their custody, or any deed or document to be taken therefrom, without the authority in writing of one Trustee and two Directors.

AUDITORS.

There shall be two Auditors, and   shall be the first and present Auditors.

The Auditors shall remain in office one year, and be eligible for re-election at the Annual Meeting.

The Accounts shall be audited, and a Balance-sheet, showing the true state of the Society's affairs, shall be signed by the Auditors, prior to every Annual Meeting; and each Auditor shall be allowed for auditing the accounts such a sum not exceeding   as the Board of Directors shall, previously to the accounts being submitted for examination, determine.

OFFICERS.

Any Officer of this Society shall, if required by the Board, give security pursuant to the provisions of the 10 Geo. 4, cap. 56, sec. 11, for any property entrusted to his charge. If a charge of gross neglect, improper conduct, or incompetency be brought against the Solicitor, Surveyor, Secretary, or Treasurer, the Board of Directors shall, at a Special Meeting convened for that purpose, investigate the case in the presence of the party charged, if he desires to be present, and if they find sufficient cause they may remove such Officer by a vote of at least three-fourths of the Directors of the Society; and in case of such removal, or in case of any vacancy occurring by the resignation or death of any Officer, the Board of Directors shall elect a successor, who shall continue in office until the next General Annual Meeting, when his appointment shall either be confirmed by the votes of a majority of Members present and voting, or another person shall be elected in his place.

ADVANCES AND REPAYMENTS.

The Society will advance to its Members the value of their Shares for terms of from   to   years, repayable by monthly or quarterly contributions covering principal and interest, at the rates following, namely :—

(Here set out the rates.)

Members not being in arrear for subscriptions or fines shall be eligible to receive advances not exceeding the value of their shares ; and if they require an advance exceeding such value they must, at the time of giving notice, pay the entrance fee and half the subscriptions upon such additional number of shares as will be equivalent to the sum required.

When any Member is desirous of having an advance made to him, he shall sign and send to the Secretary an application in writing in the form set forth in the Appendix to these Rules, and at the foot or end thereof he shall set forth a statement of the several particulars mentioned at the foot or end of the said form, and such other particulars as shall from time to time be required by the Board of Directors.

Every application for advances shall be numbered and entered by the Secretary in a book to be kept for that purpose, in the order in which they are received by the Secretary, who shall report the same to the next Board of Directors, who shall instruct the Surveyor to survey the premises proposed as a security, and report the value thereof to the Board ; and all advances shall be made in rotation, according to the order in which the applications are registered in the Book. And in case the Board shall consider the property to be a sufficient security for the required advance, they shall signify to the applicant, in writing, under the hand of the Secretary, their assent to the application, subject to the contract or conditions of sale and title proving satisfactory to the Solicitor ; and shall thereupon instruct the Solicitor to examine the proposed contract or conditions of sale, and if he shall be of opinion that they are not objectionable, then to investigate the title, and report the result of his investigation to the Board ; and in case a good and marketable title shall be deduced, or such a title as the Board of Directors, by the advice of the Solicitor, think fit to accept, the Board shall authorise the required advance to be made, upon all arrears of subscriptions, fines, and other payments due from the Member requiring the same being paid up, and upon the due execution, by all proper and necessary parties, of a proper Mortgage security to the Trustees of the Society, pursuant to these Rules.

In case any Member shall require an advance to enable him to purchase real or leasehold property at a public auction, the Board of Directors, after being satisfied in manner aforesaid that the property is of sufficient value to secure the amount, and that the conditions of sale are not objectionable, may, upon payment by the Member of the Surveyor's charges for the survey, and the Solicitor's charges for examining and reporting on the conditions of sale, depute the Secretary, Solicitor, or Treasurer of the Society to attend the sale and pay the deposit, in case the Member shall be declared the purchaser, provided the price do not exceed the amount which the Board shall be willing to advance on the security of the property; or if the price shall exceed that amount, then, provided the Member shall lodge the amount of the difference in the hands of the Treasurer of the Society, before the deposit is made. And the Board of Directors shall require such personal or other security to be given by such Member to the Trustees of the Society, for the repayment of the amount of such deposit, and all expenses, in case the purchase should not be completed, and a Mortgage to the Society executed, as the Solicitor of the Society may advise.

When a Member shall require an advance for the purpose of building, the value of the land shall be ascertained by or under the direction of the Board, and the title to it investigated in like manner as in other cases; and if the Directors shall determine to make the required advance, such Member shall be entitled, upon a proper Mortgage security being executed to the Trustees of the Society, as required by these Rules, to receive the amount in such sums, and at such time or times, as the Directors may think fit and proper, but so, nevertheless, that the advances to be made from time to time shall not exceed the value of the buildings erected at the time of such advance; such value to be determined by the Surveyor of the Society. And when the buildings are finished to the satisfaction of such Surveyor, the balance of the required advance shall be paid, upon all arrears of subscriptions, fines, and other payments which shall be due to the Society from the Member entitled to the advance being paid by him.

If any Member, after receiving the first instalment of the value of his Share or Shares, shall leave the building to erect which the same shall have been advanced unfinished, or shall neglect to proceed therewith to the satisfaction of the Surveyor of the Society, the Board of Directors, after giving to such Member ten days' notice in writing, signed by the Secretary, of their intention so to do, may either sell the premises immediately or employ some person or persons to complete the same at the expense of such Member, as the Board shall deem most advantageous to the Society; and such member shall be responsible for, and make good to the Society, any loss that may accrue in consequence.

MORTGAGES.

Whenever the value of a Share or Shares shall be advanced to any Member out of the funds of the Society, pursuant to these Rules, the property shall be secured to the Society by way of Mortgage until the amount of such Share or Shares shall be repaid to the Society, with all fines and other payments incurred in respect thereof; and every such Mortgage Deed shall be made in such form, and contain such clauses, provisoes, and agreements as the Solicitor for the Society shall think fit.

INSURANCE.

In case any Member having executed a Mortgage to the Society for the value of his Share or Shares, shall make default in payment of the expenses which the Trustees may incur in and about insuring and keeping insured the mortgaged premises with interest thereon, pursuant to the covenant in the Mortgage, he shall be liable to pay, and shall pay to the Society the same fines as he would have incurred for the non-payment of an equal amount of subscriptions at the time appointed for payment thereof.

In case of damage by fire, the Trustees of the Society for the time being shall receive from the Insurance Office the amount payable in respect of such damage, and their receipt, countersigned by the Treasurer of the Society, shall be a sufficient discharge to the Insurance Office for the money therein expressed to be received; and the Board of Directors shall have full power to settle and adjust with the Insurance Office any question relating to such insurance, and to fix the amount to be paid by the Insurance Office in respect of the damage done to the premises, or to make such arrangement with the Insurance Office as to the rebuilding or repairing of the said premises, or relating thereto, as the Board of Directors shall think reasonable.

The Board of Directors shall at their discretion either lay out the money which shall be received from any Insurance

Office as aforesaid, or any part thereof, in repairing the damage done to the premises, or retain and apply the same, or such part thereof as they shall think fit, in or towards payment and satisfaction of the amount which shall be due and owing from the Mortgagor to the Society, and pay the surplus, if any, to the Mortgagor, or to such other person as he or she shall by writing direct to receive the same.

PENALTIES FOR INVALIDATING POLICIES.

Every Member executing a Mortgage to this Society shall, within two days from the time of such execution, give to the Secretary a written statement of any trade carried on in or upon any part of the premises comprised in such Mortgage, or of the existence of any stove or furnace erected thereon, or other matter or thing which would in any way affect the validity of the policy of assurance, and if at any subsequent period any such trade shall be commenced, or erection made, the like statement shall be given ; and the Member neglecting to give such statement shall pay a fine at the discretion of the Board of not more than Ten Shillings but not less than One Shilling per week for each Share ; and the Board of Directors shall, if they think fit so to do, at least once in every year appoint some competent person to obtain all the information he can with respect to trades, &c., carried on in and about the mortgaged premises, and to report to the Board accordingly.

GROUND RENT.

Whenever any property mortgaged to the Society shall be subject to any chief or ground-rent, the Mortgagor shall from time to time produce to the Secretary a receipt for the same within seven days after the same shall become due, or in default thereof the Mortgagor shall pay a fine of Five Shillings ; and in case the rent shall not be duly paid within such period of seven days, the Board of Directors may direct the sum to be paid by the Treasurer out of the funds of the Society, and the Mortgagor shall repay the amount at the next monthly Subscription Meeting, together with a further sum of   per Share, by way of fine ; and in default of payment thereof accordingly, he shall be fined as for an equal amount of subscriptions in arrear.

SALE OF MORTGAGED PROPERTY BY MORTGAGOR.

If any Member who shall have executed a Mortgage to the Society shall be desirous of selling the mortgaged property, subject to the Mortgage, he shall be at liberty so to do, with the consent of the Board of Directors, upon first duly transferring the Shares secured by such Mortgage to the intended purchaser, in manner provided by these Rules, and upon such transfer being completed, and all arrears due to the Society from the Mortgagor being paid, and the conveyance to the purchaser executed, such purchaser shall thenceforth become liable to pay all subscriptions payable in respect of such shares, and the Board of Directors, or the Trustees, by their direction, may grant to the original Mortgagor, at his costs and charges, a release from all future liability in respect thereof.

Every such conveyance to a purchaser, subject to the Mortgage, shall be perused and settled by the Solicitor of the Society at the expense of the Mortgagor, and shall, when executed, be delivered to the Solicitor of the Society, and by him deposited with the other Title Deeds relating to the property comprised therein, as a further security for the moneys secured by the Mortgage.

POWER TO REDEEM.

If any Member who shall have executed a Mortgage to the Society shall be desirous of paying off or redeeming the same, it shall be lawful for him so to do on giving a notice of two clear calendar months prior to the ordinary Meeting at which the redemption of such Mortgage is proposed to be completed, and on payment of all advance repayments and any fines due in respect thereof, up to the time of the redemption of such Mortgage, and of the present value of the future repayments calculated by the consulting Actuary, upon the same principle as provided for such Mortgage Deed in case of a sale of the property, to the end of the original term, and discounted after a rate of interest to be fixed by the consulting Actuary, not lower than $3\frac{1}{2}$ per cent., together with a redemption fee of 5s. per cent. on the balance so due, the Trustees for the time being shall at the request of the Board of Directors, and at the cost of the Member, cause to be endorsed upon the Mortgage Deed a receipt in the form set forth in the Schedule hereto, signed by the Trustees of the Society, and all other Deeds and Documents relating to the mortgaged property, shall be delivered up to such Mortgagor. The fee payable to the consulting Actuary is to be paid by the Member.

REGISTER OF SHARES.

A Share Register Book shall be kept by the Secretary, in which shall be entered in columns the christian and surname, place of residence, profession or business, and date of entrance of each Member of the Society, and the number of Shares held by each Member, with the number and amount of each Share, and the time when the subscription for each Share commenced; and each Member shall sign his name in an appropriate column of such Share Register Book, in testimony of the accuracy of such entries respectively.

CHANGE OF RESIDENCE.

Any Member who shall change his place of abode, shall within one month afterwards give notice in writing thereof, and of his new place of abode, to the Secretary, in order that his new place of abode may be registered in the Share Register Book, and at the monthly Subscription Meeting next after such notice shall or ought to have been given, such Member shall pay to the Secretary a Register Fee of   per Share. And in case any Member shall neglect to give such notice as aforesaid, within the period hereinbefore limited for that purpose, he shall at the next monthly Subscription Meeting pay to the Secretary a fine of   per Share.

MARRIAGE OF FEMALE MEMBERS.

Any female Member who shall marry shall within one month afterwards give notice in writing thereof, and of the christian and surname, place of abode, and profession or business of her husband; and at or before the monthly Meeting of the Society next after such marriage the Shares of such female Member shall be duly transferred into the name of her husband, and upon such transfer the same Fees or Fines shall be payable as in other cases of transfer of Shares.

And in case such notice as aforesaid shall not be given within the period above limited for that purpose, a fine of   per Share shall be paid by such Member to the Society, and a further fine of   per Share, for every month which shall elapse after such notice shall or ought to have been given, until the Shares of such Member shall be duly transferred to the husband.

DEATH.

Upon the death of any Member of the Society holding Shares upon which no advance shall have been made, his legal personal representative shall within one month after his death give notice thereof in writing to the Secretary, stating the christian and surname, place of abode, and profession or business of such legal personal representative, in order that such Shares may be registered in the name of such legal personal representative, or of such other person or persons entitled thereto as he or she shall by such notice direct, or in default thereof shall pay a fine of   per Share to the Secretary; and upon such notice being given, the Shares of such deceased Member shall be transferred into the name of such legal personal representative, or into the name of such other person or persons entitled thereto as such representative shall direct, and the same Fees shall be payable upon such transfer as upon any other transfer of Shares ; and in case such Shares or any of them shall not be transferred as aforesaid, at or before the second monthly Subscription Meeting next after the death of such Member, a fine of   per Share shall be paid to the Society for every monthly Subscription Meeting after the first week shall elapse before such transfer shall have been made.

TRANSFER OF SHARES.

Any Member shall be at liberty to transfer all or any of his Shares to any other Member of the Society, or to any other person desirous of becoming a Member, upon giving to the Secretary seven days' notice in writing prior to a monthly Subscription Meeting of his intention so to do, such notice containing the christian and surname, place of abode, and profession or business of the proposed Transferee, and the number and amount of each Share proposed to be transferred, and the amount of the consideration to be paid or given by the Transferee for such transfer ; and at the first monthly meeting next after the service of such notice, a transfer of the Share or Shares specified in such notice, in the form set forth in the Schedule hereto, shall be endorsed upon the original certificate of Shares and signed by the Transferer and also by the Transferee, and deposited in the hands of the Secretary. And thereupon all arrears of subscriptions, fines, and other payments due from such Member being first paid, such Share or Shares shall be transferred into the name of the Transferee in the Share Register Book of the Society, and the Transferee shall sign his acceptance of such Share or Shares in an appropriate column of the said book, and a fee of   per Share shall at the same time be paid to the Society by the Transferee ; and upon such payment being made the Secretary shall within seven days deliver to the Transferee a new certificate or certificates of such Shares.

WITHDRAWALS.

Any person who shall have been a Member of the Society for six months, and shall not have received any advance out of the funds of the Society, shall be at liberty to withdraw from the Society upon any monthly Subscription Meeting, upon giving to the Secretary one month's previous notice in writing of his intention, and upon payment to the Secretary at the time of serving such notice of a fine of   per Share, and the full amount then due from such Member for subscriptions, fines, and other payments.

But the Board of Directors shall have full power, from time to time, to limit the number of Shares that shall be withdrawn in any one month, and all applications for advances shall have priority over notices of withdrawal.

The sum per share to be paid to any Member on his withdrawal from the Society, at any monthly Subscription Meeting, is specified in the table at the end of this Rule.

The legal personal representatives, widows, and guardians of infant children of deceased Members entitled to the Shares of such deceased Members, and the guardians or committees of Members becoming lunatic or of unsound mind, shall have priority over other Members in withdrawing from the Society.

And in case any Member shall become lunatic or of unsound mind, and no guardian or committee shall have been legally appointed, it shall be lawful for the Board of Directors to direct payment of the amount to which such Member would have been entitled on withdrawal from the Society to the person maintaining such Member, at the expiration of six months after a request in writing, signed by such person, shall have been left with the Secretary, upon satisfactory evidence being given to the Board of the lunacy or unsoundness of mind of the Member, and that he has been maintained during that period by the person so applying, and upon payment of all arrears of subscriptions, fines, and other payments payable to the Society in respect of such Shares, and upon such person giving to the Trustees of the Society such indemnity against all claims in respect of such Shares as the Board shall think fit to require for the security of the Society.

COMPULSORY WITHDRAWALS.

Whenever there is any balance in the hands of the Bankers, not wanted for advances or other claims, the Board of Directors may require the Members of the Society who have not received advances to withdraw by ballot the value of as many Shares as shall be sufficient to exhaust such balance, or so much thereof as they shall think it expedient to have withdrawn.

In balloting for such withdrawal each share shall be drawn separately, and no Member shall be compelled to withdraw the value of a second Share until every other Member shall have withdrawn one.

VOTING.

All elections and questions at any meeting shall be decided by a majority of votes, to be taken openly; and when the votes are equal the Chairman of the Meeting shall have a casting vote.

No Member shall be entitled to attend any meeting of the Society, or to vote on any question, without producing his certificate of Shares, if required so to do by the Secretary or any Member present at such Meeting.

When the conduct or affairs of any officer or Member are under discussion at any meeting of the Society, such may be present; but he may not be present when the votes are taken.

CONTINGENT FUND.

All monies received for copies of Rules, fines, fees, and other things (except monthly subscription and redemption money) shall be carried by the Secretary to the credit of an account to be entitled 'The Contingent Fund.' And all expenses for printing, rent of offices, salaries, and other outgoings (except advances and withdrawals) shall be charged to the debit of the same account in the books of the Society.

LEGAL PROCEEDINGS.

No legal proceedings shall be commenced by or on behalf of the Society against any person whomsoever without the sanction of a special meeting of the Board of Directors.

SERVICE OF NOTICES.

Service of any notice, by leaving the same at the place inserted in the Share Register Book of the Society, as the place of residence of any Member, or by sending the same by post addressed to the Member at such place, shall be deemed good service upon such Member.

FINES.

The fines for the non-payment of monthly subscriptions at the time and place appointed, or to be from time to time appointed for payment thereof, shall be Sixpence per month per Share for the first month the subscription shall be in arrear;

E

One Shilling per month per Share for the second month ; One Shilling and Sixpence for the third month ; and so on, increasing in the same proportion every month. And when the Fines which a Member has incurred shall equal the amount of the Subscriptions paid by him, the Share or Shares of such Member shall become forfeited to the Society, and he shall thenceforth cease to have any interest in the funds of the Society in respect of such Shares.

But the Board of Directors shall have power to remit or waive such forfeiture upon payment by the Member of such fine, upon such terms and conditions as they in their discretion shall think fit.

RE-CONVEYANCE.

The Trustees for the time being shall, on the withdrawal of any Member, and when all advances and other payments have been repaid by him, at the cost of the several Members requiring the same, indorse upon every Mortgage given to the Society by such Members respectively, a receipt for all monies intended to be secured thereby, in the form in the Schedule pursuant to the 6 and 7 William IV., cap. 32, sec. 5, and shall deliver up the same, with all other deeds and documents which shall have been deposited with them by such Member.

ARBITRATION.

The Board of Directors shall determine all questions which may arise upon the construction of the rules of the Society, and also all matters in difference between any Member of the Society, relating to the Society, or between any Member and any officer of the Society, if the parties shall consent in writing to submit to their decision, and such decision shall be final ; but if otherwise, reference shall be made to arbitration, pursuant to 10 Geo. IV., cap. 56, sec. 27.

At the first meeting of the Society after the enrolment of these Rules, five Arbitrators shall be elected—none of the said Arbitrators being beneficially interested, directly or indirectly, in the funds of the Society—and in each case of dispute the names of the Arbitrators shall be written on pieces of paper, and placed in a box, and the three whose names are first drawn by the complaining party, or by some one appointed by such party, shall be Arbitrators to decide the matters in difference, whose decision shall be final and binding on all parties. The costs of the reference shall be paid by such party, or by the parties in such proportions as the Arbitrators shall direct. The party requiring the arbitration shall deposit with the Secretary a sum to be fixed by the Board of Directors to compensate the Arbitrators for their trouble.

RULES.

Every Member, on joining the Society, shall pay for a copy of the Rules.

No addition to, alteration in, or repeal of these or any future Rules shall be made, unless at a General Meeting of the Society convened for that purpose, by giving to each member seven days' notice of the time, and place, and object thereof, and in pursuance of a requisition by seven Members, and addressed to the Secretary, specifying the addition, alteration, or repeal proposed to be made, which requisition shall be publicly read at two regular Monthly Subscription Meetings of the Society, held next before such General Meeting; and no such addition, alteration, or repeal shall be made but with the concurrence of three-fourths of the Members present at such General Meeting.

In the construction of the Rules, unless there be something in the subject or context repugnant to such construction, every word importing the singular number only shall mean and include several persons or things, as well as one person or thing, and the converse; and every word importing the masculine gender only shall mean and include a female as well as a male, and the words 'month' and 'monthly' shall mean a calendar and not a lunar month.

SCHEDULE.

FORMS REFERRED TO IN THE FOREGOING RULES.

No. 1.—SHARE CERTIFICATE.

Share.   Register No.

This is to certify that   of   is the proprietor of one   share, of the value of £   in the capital stock of the   Benefit Building Society, subject to the payment of subscriptions and other liabilities according to the rules of the society, which may from time to time be in force.

As witness our hands this   day of   one thousand eight hundred and   (date of taking up the share) counter signed.

Secretary.   Directors.

E 2

No. 2.—NOTICE OF SALE BY AUCTION.

To the Secretary of the   *Benefit Building Society.*

I, the undersigned, being a member of the above Society, and having obtained   advances of   on my shares in this Society, wish to purchase, according to the rules of the said Society, lot   specified in the particulars of sale herewith forwarded. I therefore hereby request you to let the solicitor peruse them on my behalf, and if he shall consider the particulars such as it would be prudent to purchase under, to give notice to the surveyor of the Society, to examine and report as to the eligibility of the property comprised in the lot before mentioned. And I hereby request that the said opinions be laid before the directors, and that they will authorise the money required as a deposit to be advanced in part payment of the purchase money, in case the aforesaid lot shall be declared to have been purchased by me, within the limits specified in the reports of the solicitor and surveyor.

Dated,   Signed,   Register No.
               Residence,

No. 3.—NOTICE TO TRANSFER SHARES.

To the Secretary of the   *Benefit Building Society.*

I,   being a member of the above Society, hereby give you notice that it is my wish to transfer my shares in the above Society, to   for the sum of £ and I request you to lay this application before the board of directors for their consideration.

Signed,   Residence,   Register No.

No. 4.—TRANSFER OF SHARES.

I,   of   in the county of   one of the shareholders of the   Benefit Building Society, in consideration of the sum of   sterling paid to me by   hereby assign and transfer to the said his executors, administrators, and assigns,   shares of and in the funds of the said association, to hold the same unto the said   his executors, administrators, and assigns, subject to the payments, rules, and regulations of the society, and I, the said   do hereby agree to accept the said shares if admitted a member, subject to the same payments, rules, and regulations. As witness our hands and seals this   day of   one thousand eight hundred and

Name of original member,   No.
Residence,
Name of purchaser,
Residence,

___

No. 5.—APPLICATION FOR ADVANCES.

To the Secretary of the   *Benefit Building Society.*

I,   being a member of the above Society, registered No.   hereby request you to register my name in the application book, as being desirous to receive advances on my shares subscribed for in this institution, on or about the   day of 18   I hold   shares, and it is my wish to take up additional shares. Dated this   day of one thousand eight hundred and

                   Signed,
                   Residence,

___

No. 6.—RECEIPT TO BE ENDORSED ON SATISFIED MORTGAGES.

We whose names are hereunder written, being trustees of the within-named Society, do hereby acknowledge to have received from   all monies intended to be secured by the within written deed, as witness our hands this day of

___

No. 7.—PARTICULARS FOR BUILDING ADVANCES.

Member's Name,   Residence,
        Occupation,   Register No.
Date of Admission,   Application No.   Date,
Situation of land,   No. of square yards,
If freehold or leasehold,   Price per yard,
If leasehold, is it an under lease,
          Date of lease,   for what number of years,
How many unexpired,
Name of owner,   Residence,
Amount of ground rent,
         when payable,   to whom payable,
If the land is subject to any other payments besides the ground rent,
Covenants of lease,
Nature of the buildings to be erected,
        Total estimated cost,
Name of architect furnishing the plans,
Name of builder,
No. of shares now held,
        Amount of advances required,

Additional shares to be taken up,
Total weekly or monthly payment,
　　　　Amount paid in to this date,
Report of inspecting directors,
Report of solicitor on title deeds,
Report of surveyor on land and proposed buildings,
Time of commencing the building,
When considered by the directors,
　　　　Amount to be advanced,　　　　　Minute No.
Cost of lease,
Solicitor's charges,
Surveyor's charges,
Insurance,
Question to member :—When the solicitor of the Society has
　　prepared the mortgage deeds, shall you wish to submit
　　them to your solicitor ?

　　When the member intends to furnish his own plans for
building, it is desirable that he should produce a plan and particulars of the position of the property, the streets, drains,
boundaries, and contents in superficial yards, the cardinal
points, and the names of the owners of the adjoining property ;
also a basement plan with drains marked ; a plan of the ground
floor of the house, showing the privies and yards ; a plan of
the chamber floor ; a front elevation of the building ; and a
detailed specification of work proposed to be done.

N. B.—A similar form to the above will be used when pro-
　　perties or land are about to be purchased.

No. 8.—Notice of Withdrawal.

　　I,　　　　　　　　　residing　　　　　　　Register No.
in the　　　　　　　Benefit Building Society, do hereby give you
notice that it is my desire to withdraw the amount paid
by me on my　　　　　share　　　numbered　　　　　from the
said society, and request that you will duly lay this notice
before the directors.
　　　　　　　Name,
　　　　　　　Date,

MORTGAGE IN FEE TO THE TRUSTEES OF A BENEFIT BUILDING SOCIETY.

This Indenture, made   , between A. B., of   (hereinafter referred to as the 'mortgagor'), of the one part, and C. D., of   , E. F., of   , and G. H., of   , Trustees of the   Benefit Building Society, established under the provisions of the Act, the 6th and 7th William the 4th, cap. 32, (hereinafter referred to as the 'mortgagees') of the other part.

Whereas the said mortgagor is seized of or entitled to the hereditaments hereafter mentioned, and intended to be hereby granted for an estate of inheritance in fee simple, in possession free from incumbrances; And whereas the said mortgagor is a member of the said Society, and has subscribed for   shares therein, and by the rules of the said Society he is entitled to receive out of the funds thereof an advance of £   (being the value of his said shares) for the term of   years, repayable by monthly (or quarterly) contributions of £   to be secured in manner hereinafter appearing: Now this Indenture witnesseth that in consideration of the sum of £   to the said mortgagor in hand, paid by the said mortgagees out of the funds of the said Society, the receipt whereof, and that the same is in full satisfaction and discharge of his said shares in the said Society, he the said mortgagor doth hereby acknowledge; He the said mortgagor doth hereby for himself, his heirs, executors, and administrators, covenant with the said mortgagees, that he the said mortgagor, his heirs, executors, or administrators, will at all times hereafter during the said term of   years, pay to the trustees or trustee for the time being of the said Society, the several monthly (or quarterly) contributions or sums of money which under or by virtue of the rules for the time being of the said Society, shall become due and payable by the said mortgagor, in respect of the said advance, and will make all such payments without any deduction, and in the manner and at the place prescribed by the rules for the time being of the said Society; and will at all times hereafter observe and perform all and every the same rules in relation to the said shares and advance, and to the premises hereinbefore expressed to be hereby granted. And this Indenture also witnesseth that for the consideration aforesaid, he the said mortgagor doth hereby grant and convey unto the said mortgagees, their heirs and assigns, all (*parcels*) together with their rights, easements, known or reputed appurtenances, and all the estate and interest of the said A. B. in, to, and out of the said premises; To hold the said premises unto and to the use of the said mortgagees, their heirs and assigns, subject to the proviso for redemption hereinafter contained : Provided always, and it is hereby agreed and declared, that if the said mortgagor, his heirs, executors, administrators, or assigns, shall at all times hereafter during the said term of   years pay to the trustees or trustee for the time being of the said Society, the several monthly (or quarterly) contributions or sums of money which under or by virtue of the rules for the time being of the said Society shall become due, and payable in respect of the said advance, and shall make all such payments without any deduction and in the manner and at the place prescribed by the rules for the time being of the said Society, and observe and perform all the same rules ; then the said mortgagees shall endorse upon these presents a receipt for all monies intended to be hereby secured.   And it is hereby provided and declared, that the said mortgagees may at any time or times hereafter, without any further consent on the part of the said mortgagor, his heirs or assigns, enter into the possession or into the receipt of the rents of the said premises, and also let the same, and at the cost and sole risk of the said mortgagor appoint a person to collect the rents of the said premises for the use and benefit of the said Society at such commission as the mortgagees shall think fit ; and also, at any time or times hereafter, sell all or any part of the said premises either by public auction or private contract, and either together or in lots, with full power to buy in or rescind any contract for sale, and to resell without being responsible for any loss which may be occasioned thereby : Provided nevertheless that none of the said powers shall be executed until default shall have been made for one calendar month in payment of some monthly (or quarterly) contribution or sum of money hereinbefore covenanted to be paid, or in the observance or performance of some of the rules for the time being of the said Society or of the covenants herein contained : Provided also, that upon any sale purporting to be made in pursuance of the aforesaid power, no purchaser shall be bound to enquire whether the case mentioned in the clause lastly hereinbefore contained has happened, nor whether any money remains upon the security of these presents, nor as to the propriety or regularity of such sale ; and notwithstanding any impropriety or irregularity whatsoever in any such sale, the same shall, as regards the purchaser or purchasers, be deemed to be within the aforesaid power, and be valid accordingly. And it is hereby declared that the said mortgagees shall hold the monies to arise from the exercise of any of the aforesaid powers, upon trust, in the first place thereout to pay all the expenses incurred in or about the execution of any of the powers or trusts herein contained ; and in the next place to apply such monies in or towards payment not only of all sums of money then due and unpaid to the said Society, whether for contributions, fines, or otherwise, but also of the then present value of all the then future monthly (or quarterly) contributions herein-before covenanted to be paid, the then present value of such future payments to be calculated by the consulting Actuary of the said Society, from the date of the completion of the sale or sales to the end of the said term of   years, discount being allowed at a rate to be fixed by the said Actuary, not exceeding $3\frac{1}{2}$ per cent. per annum, on such future repayments to the end of the said term, and upon the principal of repay-ments made at the end of each year, and then to pay the surplus (if any) of the monies to arise from such sale and the rents and profits until sale, to the said mortgagor, his heirs and assigns ; And the said mortgagor, for 'himself, his heirs, executors, and administrators, hereby covenants with the said mortgagees that in case the said rents and profits and the monies to arise from the sale of the said premises shall not be sufficient to pay the monies due to the said Society, and the value of the said future contributions, then he the said mortgagor, his heirs, executors, administrators, or assigns, will, on demand, pay unto the trustees or trustee for the time being of the said Society, the amount of such deficiency as aforesaid, together with in-terest thereon after the rate of £6 per cent. per annum, from the time of the completion of the sale of the premises. And the said mortgagor doth hereby for himself, his heirs, executors, and administrators, covenant with the said mortgagees, that he, the said mortgagor, now hath power to grant all the said pre-mises to the use of the said mortgagees, their heirs and assigns, in manner aforesaid, free from incumbrances; And that he, the said mortgagor, and his heirs, and all other persons law-fully or equitably claiming any estate or interest in the premises, will, at all times, at the request of the said mortgagees, but at the cost, until foreclosure or sale, of the said mortgagor, and afterwards of the person or persons requiring the same, execute and do every such lawful assurance and thing, for the further or more perfectly assuring all or any of the said pre-mises to the use of the said mortgagees, their heirs and assigns, as by them shall be reasonably required.

Provided always,* that if the mortgagees shall at any time, by virtue of these presents or of the rules for the time being of the said Society, become entitled to enter into possession or receipt of the rents of the said premises, and the said mortgagor shall then or afterwards be in the occupation of the whole or part of the said premises, he shall during such occupation be deemed to be tenant thereof at the will of the mortgagees at a clear monthly rent of £   , payable to the mortgagees monthly in

---

* For a regular attornment clause see next precedent.

E 3

advance at the place where, and on the days and during the hours when, the monthly meetings of the said Society shall from time to time be held, and the first payment of such rent shall become due on the day on which the mortgagees shall first become entitled to enter into such possession or receipt, but every payment actually made of such rent shall be accepted by the mortgagees in or towards satisfaction of the subscriptions and monies for the time being payable by the mortgagor under the said rules and these presents respectively. And lastly, it is hereby agreed and declared that the expression 'the mortgagor' hereinbefore contained shall be construed to include and shall signify 'his heirs and assigns,' and that the expression 'the mortgagees' shall be construed to include and shall signify the survivors and survivor of them, or other the trustees or trustee for the time being of the said Society, and that all powers hereinbefore given to the mortgagees shall be exercisable by the said trustees or trustee for the time being. In witness, &c.

MORTGAGE OF LEASEHOLDS TO A BENEFIT BUILDING SOCIETY BY DEMISE.

This Indenture, made the　　　day of　　　, between A. B., of　　　hereinafter referred to as 'the mortgagor,' of the one part, and C. D. of　　　, E. F. of　　　, and G. H. of　　　, Trustees of the　　　Benefit Building Society, established under the provisions of the Act, the 6 and 7 William IV. cap. 32 (hereinafter referred to as 'the mortgagees'), of the other part:

Whereas the said mortgagor is entitled to the premises hereinafter described for the residue of the term of　　　years granted by a certain indenture, &c. And whereas the said mortgagor is a member, &c. (*as in last precedent*).—Now this indenture witnesseth that in consideration of the sum of £　　, &c. (*covenant for payment of subscriptions, as in last precedent*). And this indenture also witnesseth that for the consideration aforesaid the mortgagor hereby demises to the mortgagees, their executors, administrators, and assigns, all (*parcels*) with the actual and reputed easements and appurtenances, to hold the same unto the mortgagees, their executors, administrators, and assigns, for the residue of the said term of　　　years (except the last day thereof), subject to the proviso for redemption hereinafter contained (*proviso for redemption, as in last precedent*). And it is hereby agreed, that at any time during the continuance of this security the mortgagees may, without any further consent on the part of the mortgagor, enter into the possession or receipt of the rents of the premises, and may appoint a receiver of the said rents, who shall be deemed the agent of the mortgagor, but shall pay the rents received to the mortgagees, and may lease the said premises for the purpose of occupation for any term not exceeding twenty-one years in possession at rack rent, or for building or repairing purposes for any longer term in possession at the best rent which under the circumstances can reasonably be obtained without taking a premium, and may, in case they shall in their discretion think fit, sell the premises or any part thereof, &c. (*as in last precedent*).

Provided (*powers not to be exercised until default—purchasers' indemnity clause—application of sale monies—see last precedent*). And the said mortgagor hereby agrees, that after any sale under the said power of sale he will hold the said last day of the said term in the premises sold upon trust for the purchaser or purchasers thereof. And this indenture also witnesseth, that the said mortgagor doth hereby attorn and become tenant, from month to month, to the mortgagees for and in respect of all the said premises at a monthly rent of one pepper corn until default shall have been made in payment of some subscription or money which under the said rules or these presents shall become payable in respect of the said advance, or otherwise under this security, and afterwards at a clear monthly rent of such a sum as shall be equal or amount to the monies payable monthly by the mortgagor from time to time for subscriptions, repayments, and fines under the said rules, and that such monthly rent shall become due monthly in advance, and shall be payable at the place on the day and during the hours where and when the monthly meetings of the said Society shall from time to time be held, and the first payment thereof shall be made on such of the said days as shall occur next after any such subscription repayment or fine shall have become in arrear; but all monies received by the said mortgagees for rent under the attornment hereinbefore contained shall be accepted in or towards satisfaction of the subscriptions, repayments, fines and monies then in arrear, or payable under the said rules and these presents respectively. And the mortgagor hereby for himself and his heirs covenants with the mortgagees, their executors, administrators, and assigns, that the said indenture of lease is subsisting and valid; and that the rent thereby reserved, and the lessee's covenants therein contained, have been paid and performed up to the present date; and that he now has power to demise the said premises to the mortgagees, their executors, administrators, and assigns, for the term and in the manner hereinbefore expressed, and free from all incumbrances; and further, that if the mortgagees shall become entitled under these presents to enter into possession or receipt of the rents of or to lease or sell the said premises under the powers hereinbefore contained, it shall be lawful for them, their executors, administrators, and assigns, to enter into and thenceforth to continue in possession or receipt of the rents of the said premises without any interruption, claim, or demand ; and further, that the mortgagor, and every person having or claiming any estate or interest in the said premises, will at all times (at the cost of the mortgagor until and upon a sale under the power of sale hereinbefore contained, and afterwards of the person or persons requiring the same) execute and do every such assurance and thing for more effectually assuring the said premises to the mortgagees (and for assigning if when and as required the last day of the said term and the premises therein comprised unto the mortgagees, or as they shall direct) as by them shall reasonably be required ; and further, that the mortgagor will during the continuance of this security, and whether the mortgagees shall or shall not be in possession or receipt of the rents of the premises, pay the rent reserved by and perform all the lessee's covenants contained in the said indenture of lease, and indemnify the mortgagees against the nonpayment or nonperformance thereof; and lastly, it is hereby declared that the expression the mortgagor hereinbefore used shall be construed to include and shall signify his executors, administrators, and assigns, and that the expression the mortgagees shall be construed to include and shall signify the survivors and survivor of them or other the trustees for the time being of the said Society, and that all powers hereinbefore given to the mortgagees shall be exercisable by the said trustees or trustee for the time being.

FURTHER CHARGE TO A BUILDING SOCIETY IN RESPECT OF ADDITIONAL SHARES BY INDORSEMENT ON THE MORTGAGE DEED.

This Indenture, made the   day of 18   , between the within-named A. B. (hereinafter referred to as ' the mortgagor '), of the first part, and the within-named C. D. and G. H. and I. K. of &c., the present trustees of the within-named Society (hereinafter referred to as ' the mortgagees '), of the second part, witnesseth that in consideration of £   now paid out of the funds of the said Society by the mortgagees to the mortgagor, being the amount to which he is entitled in respect of   additional shares held by him in the funds of the said Society (the receipt whereof he hereby acknowledges), the mortgagor hereby for himself and his heirs covenants with the mortgagees that he will duly and punctually pay to the trustees or trustee for the time being of the said Society all subscriptions and other monies which shall from time to time become payable in respect of the said   shares according to the rules for the time being of the said Society; and it is hereby agreed and declared, and the mortgagor hereby for himself and his heirs covenants with the said mortgagees, their executors, administrators, and assigns, that all and singular the tenements and hereditaments by the within-written indenture expressed to be assured shall be and remain a security for and stand charged with the payment to the trustees or trustee for the time being of the said Society, of as well the subscriptions and other monies which shall from time to time become payable in respect of the said   additional shares according to the rules for the time being of the said Society, as the subscriptions and other monies which shall from time to time become payable in respect of the   shares mentioned in the within-written indenture according to the said rules, and shall not be redeemed or redeemable but upon payment of the whole of the said several subscriptions and monies accordingly.   And that all the powers in the within-written indenture contained for better securing the payment of the subscriptions and other monies intended to be thereby secured, and all trusts and provisions ancillary or relating thereto, shall extend and be applicable to secure the payment of the subscriptions and other monies hereinbefore covenanted to be paid, and that the expressions the mortgagor and the the mortgagees herein used shall be constructed in a similar manner to the same expressions in the within-written indenture. In witness, &c.

CASES.

Payne, *Ex parte*, 5 Dowl. & L. 13 Jur. 634.—*By the rules of a Building Society, duly enrolled under the 6 & 7 Will. 4, s. 32, it was provided that all matters of dispute should be preferred to two of Her Majesty's justices of the peace, in pursuance of the provisions of the 10 Geo. 4, c. 56, s. 27. Held, on motion for a mandamus to the judge of one of the county courts, to proceed and hear a plaint levied by one of the members against the officer of the society, that the jurisdiction of the county court did not extend to any disputes arising between the members of any such societies.*

This was a rule calling upon a judge of the county court of Bedfordshire to show cause why a *mandamus* should not issue, commanding him to hear a plaint in a cause of *Payne* v. *Garratt.* The following were the facts as they appeared from the affidavit, The plaintiff Payne was a member of a certain building society, duly enrolled under the 6 & 7 Will. 4, c. 32, and the defendant Garrat was a trustee or officer of the said society. Among the rules was one (rule 25), that all matters of dispute be referred to two of Her Majesty's justices of the peace, according to the provisions of the 10 Geo. 4, c. 26, s. 27. In consequence of certain disputes that had risen, Payne withrew from the society, and then levied a plaint in the county court for his share, which was under £20. The judge, considering that he had no jurisdiction to entertain the matter, refused to hear the plaint whereupon the present rule was obtained.

WIGHTMAN, J.—Upon a rule for a *mandamus* to the judge of the county court to proceed with this action, which was brought by a member of a building society, within the provisions of the 6 & 7 Will. 4, c. 32, against an officer of that society, it was contended that by sect. 4 of that statute, incorporating the provisions of the 10 Geo. 4, c. 56, ss. 27, 28, 29, and by the 25th rule of this society, directing a reference of all disputes to justices of the peace, the right to bring this action was taken away; and I am of opinion that this is so. By these sections, provision is directed to be made by the rules specifying whether disputes shall be referred to justices or to arbitrators, and the decision upon such reference is made final. These sections and this rule, providing for a cheap, simple, and speedy decision, oust the jurisdiction of the ordinary tribunals (*Crisp* v. *Bunbury, Timms* v. *Williams*, 2 Q. B. Rev. 413). In *Crabill* v. *Kingdom*, the action was held maintainable, because the rule there relating to reference did not comprise the matter of that action, but by the exception the rule was recognised. The 9 & 10 Vict. c. 95, s. 58, does not operate to take away the effect of these statutes from county courts, or revive a power of bringing actions there, which had been taken away from all courts generally. The rule, therefore, must be discharged.

Rule discharged.

Reeves and Another *v.* White, Justice of the Peace, 118.— *To a declaration by the trustees of a Building Society on the covenants of a mortgage deed given to them by a subscriber to secure the sum appropriated and lent to him by the society, the defendant pleaded that arbitrators had been appointed pursuant to the statutes in the behalf and the rules of the society ; that the claims in the declaration were matters in dispute between him and the society within the meaning of the statute and the rules, and that he had always been ready and willing, and still offered to refer the claims to arbitrators. The plaintiff replied, specially traversing the appointment of arbitrators, and stating by way of inducement that the first meeting of the society took place long before the defendant became a member ; that by accident, mistake, and oversight, arbitrators had not then been appointed, and that at the time of the accruing of the causes of action and of the commencement of the suit, there were no arbitrators. Held, that the plea was an answer to the declaration, and the replication an answer to the plea.*

A second plea set up the defence, that by the rules, the society was empowered, under the circumstances of the case, to appoint a person to collect the rents and profits of the mortgagee's premises, and reimburse the society its costs, and pay the principal and interest due ; that the rents and profits were sufficient ; that the defendant had always been willing to allow the rents and profits to be so collected and paid over, or to collect them himself and pay them over, yet the directors had not appointed any one or the defendant himself to collect and pay over, as they might and ought to have done according to the true intent and meaning of the rules and statutes. On demurrer, held, *that the society was entitled, at its option, to take the remedy suggested by the plea, or the remedy on the deed.*

Quære, whether it would have been a good plea to the declaration, to have stated that the defendant was ready and willing to refer the matters in difference to arbitration, according to the rules and the statutes ; that he had requested the directors to do what was necessary for that purpose, and that they had neglected to do so ?

In every case in which the remedy by arbitration under the 10 Geo. 4, c. 56, may be pursued, it is the sole remedy.

Lord CAMPBELL, C.J.—In this case we are of opinion, upon the demurrer to the replication to the first plea, there ought to be judgment for the plaintiffs. The declaration seems to us sufficient to show a right of action in the trustees of the building and investment association under the 6 & 7 Will. 4, c. 32, s. 4 and 10 Geo. 4, c. 56, s. 21. We are inclined to think the first plea is good. After setting out the 33rd rule of the society for referring the claims and cause of action in the declaration mentioned as matters of dispute between the society and the members thereof, and that the arbitrators were duly appointed according to the said rule, and continued to be arbitrators thenceforth until the commencement of this suit, it proceeds to state that the defendant has always been, and still is, ready and willing to refer the said matters in difference to the said arbitrators, according to the rule and the statute, and that the directors were not willing to do so. A mere covenant between the parties to refer to arbitration will not oust a court of law of their jurisdiction; but the question is, whether an arbitrator being duly appointed, the legislature has not enacted that all matters of difference between the society and the members shall be referred to the said arbitrator, and finally adjudicated on by him to the exclusion of any action in a court of law. In *Ex parte Payne*, 5 D. & L. 679. *Erle*, J., sitting in the Bail Court, after full argument and great deliberation, put this construction on the 27th section of 10 Geo. 4, c. 56; considering it to be the express intention of the legislature to protect such societies and their members, generally persons of an inferior rank of life with small wages, from the vexation and ruin which might be brought on them in courts of law, and to provide for them a domestic forum by which their differences might be speedily decided and at a small expense. The same construction was put on a similar statute by the Court of Common Pleas in *Crisp* v. *Bunbury*, 8 Bing. 394; in which *Tindal*, C.J., impressively pointed out the oppressive consequences which would follow to such societies and their members if this power of referring to arbitration were held to be cumulative only. The case of *Morrison* v. *Glover*, 4 Ex. R. 430, holding that an action might be maintained by the trustees of a building society, proceeded on the ground that there part of the plaintiff's claim was not matter in dispute between him and the defendant as a member; and in *Doe dem. Morrison* v. *Glover*, 12 Q. B. 103, it was held merely that an ejectment for the benefit of the building society might be maintained in the name of John Doe upon the demise of the person in whom the legal estate vested. The other authorities relied on do not show that in all cases the society has the option either to refer or to bring an action, and do not outweigh *Ex parte Payne* and *Crisp* v. *Bunbury*; and on an attentive consideration of the words of the Act of Parliament, it appears to us to be not merely permissive, but to be enacted that where there may be, there must be a reference to the arbitrators. Supposing the first plea to be sufficient, we are of opinion that it is sufficiently answered by the replication, which traverses the allegation that the arbitrators were appointed according to the rules of the society and the Act of Parliament, and the traverse shows that the arbitrator never had been appointed by the society, and that when those matters in difference arose for which the action is brought, a reference to arbitration was impossible. The defendant's counsel contended, that it was not competent to the society to take advantage of their own wrong, and that it could not be allowed to aver that arbitrators were not appointed. We are not called upon to decide what the effect would have been if the defendant, in this plea, instead of alleging that arbitrators had been appointed, had merely alleged that he was ready and willing to refer the matters in difference to arbitration according to the rule and the statute, and that he had requested in vain the directors to do what was necessary for that purpose. But we entertain no doubt that where he has alleged that the arbitrators were appointed, to whom the matters in difference might have been referred, a traverse of that allegation which is made material is a good answer to the plea. We are likewise of opinion that there must be judgment for the plaintiffs on the demurrer to the second plea, founded on the eighteenth and nineteenth rules of the society, though the directors might have a remedy by appointing a receiver of the rents, and exercising their power of sale.

Judgment for the plaintiffs.

Grinham *v.* Card, 7 Exch. Rep. 833.— *Where, by the rules of a Friendly Society, disputes between members and the trustees may be referred to the arbitration of a certain number of the committee, a dispute which affects the interests of all the individual members of the society, arising between some of its members, who are also members of the committee, and the trustees, where the question is not one which necessarily requires that recourse should be had to a court of equity, such dispute cannot be referred to the judge of the county court, but must be referred to other members of the committee.*

Where a dispute arose between two of the members of the committee of a Friendly Society and the trustees, touching the distribution of a fund in the hands of the latter, and, by one of the rules of the society, it was ordered that disputes were to be referred to such members of the committee as should not be personally interested in the matter: Held, that the judge of the county court has no jurisdiction in such case, and the court granted a prohibition against further proceedings in a plaint issued out of the court over which he presided.

Honeyman had obtained a rule, calling on the plaintiffs in a plaint of *Grinham* v. *Card*, trustees of the 'Frant Friendly Society,' and the judge of the county court of Kent, to show cause why a writ of prohibition should not issue to him to stay all further proceedings in the said plaint. It appeared from the affidavits, that the plaintiffs were two of the members of the committee of the Frant Friendly Society, and that the defendants were the trustees of that body. The particulars of the plaintiffs' demand in the said plaint were as follows :—' For you to show cause why you did not pay over the money or reserved fund of the Frant Friendly Society, in your hands or power, as trustees of the said society, as required and prescribed by a rule of the said society, duly made and passed by the said society, and certified on the 10th of July 1850.' It further appeared that the society was originally established in 1836, when, among other rules for its governance, the 32nd rule, which was duly enrolled and certified by John Tidd Pratt, Esq., was as follows :—' That if any difference or dispute shall arise between any of the members of this society, not being officers, touching any matter or thing relating to this society, it shall be referred to the committee for their decision ; but if any dispute or difference shall arise between any officers of this society, or between any other member and an officer or officers, it shall be first referred to the committee, or such of them as shall not be personally interested therein, and if the decision of such committee shall not be satisfactory to all parties concerned, then reference shall be made to arbitrators, pursuant to the 10 Geo. 4, c. 56, s. 27.' The 'reserved fund' was not established until the year 1839, and it consisted of the accumulated subscriptions of the honorary members, and its application was regulated by a rule (38), which was framed in that year. In 1847, this rule was altered, and the application of the reserved fund was also altered, and the payments were directed to be made pursuant to a certain scale. This rule provided, ' that if any difference or dispute shall arise touching this fund or the construction of this rule, the same shall be referred to arbitration in the manner specified by the rule of this society.' On the 10th of July 1850, this rule was also expunged, and the following rule was made and duly certified. This rule, after directing that rule 38 be expunged, proceeded as follows :—' And that the money now in the bank in the names of the trustees, and other monies that shall or may be due to the reserved fund, may be issued, returnable before two justices calling upon the party against whom complaint is made, to appear before them, and upon appearance or default, the justices may ' make such order thereupon as to them may seem just : and if the sum of money so awarded, together with a sum for costs not exceeding the sum of 10s. as to such justices shall seem meet, shall not be immediately paid, then the justices shall issue their distress warrant.' The provisions of the 27th section would apply to cases where an award by arbitrators for payment of money in the form given in the schedule has not been complied with, and the money has not been paid at the time specified in the award ; in such a case the proceeding before the justices would be merely to enforce payment, and, if not *immediately* paid, when the parties appear, the justices may issue a warrant of distress. There can in such case be no reason for another summons before a distress warrant issues.

But it appears to us that, if the proceedings are under the 28th section, and the justices have made an order for payment of money, analogous to the award of arbitrators under the 27th section, a distress warrant cannot issue for non-compliance with such an order, without a previous summons to the party who may have various reasons to assign against the issuing of the distress warrant. He may not have knowledge of the order, he may be ready to pay the person named in the order if he could find him, he may actually have tendered or even paid the money, all which reasonable excuses would be unavailable if the party to whom the money is ordered to be paid could, *ex parte*, and without notice, obtain a distress warrant. The recitals in the warrant in the present case state service of the order, and demand and refusal, all which might be controverted, and we therefore think, in accordance with the principle of the decision of this court in the case of *Painter* v. *Liverpool Gas Company*, 3 Ad. & El. 433, that wherever cause could be shown against issuing a warrant of distress, a previous summons is necessary. And, as no such summons was issued in this case, but the warrant was obtained *ex parte*, the rule will be absolute to enter a verdict for the plaintiff for 8l. 1s. 1d.

Rule absolute.

Reg. *v.* Grant, 13 Jur. 1026 ; 14 Q. B. Rep. 43.—*By sect.* 27 *of* 10 *Geo.* 4, *c.* 56, *relating to Friendly Societies, an award made according to the true purport and meaning of the rules of the Friendly Society shall be final and binding.* The 26th *rule of the Leeds Philanthropic Society declared that all matters in dispute between the society and any individual member should be referred to arbitration, that the arbitrators should hear evidence on both sides, and that their decision should be binding to all parties and final. By sect.* 7 *of stat.* 4 & 5 *W.* 4, *c.* 40, *jurisdiction is given to justices of the peace, in case of neglect or refusal by the arbitrators to make an award.*

P. J., a member of the Leeds Philanthropic Society, who had been expelled for an alleged breach of one of the rules of the society, applied to arbitrators duly appointed according to the statute, and they made an award that P. J. be expelled from the society. P. J., treating the award as void and null, applied to justices for the county, who made an order in which they adjudged that the arbitrators had neglected and refused to hear evidence on both sides, touching the matter in dispute, and to make their award therein, and that P. J. be reinstated in the society. Upon a rule for quashing the order,—Held, first, that the adjudication by the justices, that the arbitrators had neglected and refused to make an award, was a decision upon one of the preliminaries necessary to their jurisdiction, and therefore was not conclusive. Secondly, that as the affidavits contained sufficient to show that the justices were warranted in considering it proved that the arbitrators had wrongfully refused to hear evidence on the part of P. J., there was no final and binding award; and therefore the justices had jurisdiction to make the order.

The society was formed within the borough of Leeds, which is within the West Riding of Yorkshire, but has a court of quarter sessions and justices with exclusive jurisdiction, all meetings were held, and all the business transacted, and the award made within the borough. But the member resided, and the act with which he was charged took place, in the West Riding without the borough. Held, That the justices of the West Riding had jurisdiction to hear the complaint and make the order.

This was a rule calling upon the prosecutors to show cause why a certain order made by the justices in and for the West Riding of the county of York, dated the 11th January 1847, whereby the presidents, stewards, and members of a certain Friendly Society, called the 'Leeds Philanthropic Society,' duly established and holden at Leeds, in the West Riding, under stat. 10 Geo. 4, c. 56, were adjudged and ordered forthwith to reinstate Philemon Jacques in the said society, and readmit him to all the benefits arising therefrom accordingly, should not be quashed for insufficiency.

Lord DENMAN, C.J., in delivering the judgment of the court, said:—On a motion to quash an order of justices brought up by *certiorari*, it appeared by the affidavits that the complainant had applied to arbitrators duly appointed according to the statute; that they had, in fact, made an award between the complainant and the Friendly Society; that the complainant, treating the award as void and null, had then applied to justices, who made the order in question, and therein declared that the arbitrators had neglected and omitted to make any award, this being the condition on which their jurisdiction to take cognizance of the dispute depends.

Upon these facts the question has been, whether the statement in the order that the arbitrators had neglected and omitted to make an award was conclusive. It is clear that the decision of a tribunal lawfully constituted, upon a question properly brought before it respecting a matter within its jurisdiction, is not open to review by *certiorari* ; *Reg.* v. *Bolton*, 1 Q. B. 66, 5 Jur. 1154 ; but the decision of persons assuming to be a tribunal, that they are lawfully constituted, is open to review. In the present case, the justices are in the nature of two arbitrators, the reference being conditional upon the first arbitrators neglecting or omitting to award ; and their decision that this condition existed is a decision upon one of the preliminaries necessary for constituting them a lawful tribunal for this matter. It is therefore not conclusive within the principle laid down in *Reg.* v. *Bolton.* 1 Q. B. 66, 5 Jur. 1154, but falls within the latter of the two limitations of it there mentioned, namely, where the charge is really insufficient, but is misstated in drawing up the proceedings, so that they appear regular. In such case it is competent to the defendant to show by affidavit what the real charge was, and if that shows that the magistrates ought never to have begun the inquiry, the order is to be quashed.

We have therefore in the present case found it our duty to inquire, whether the statement in the order respecting the neglect and refusal of the arbitrators to make an award was true. The admitted facts are, that arbitrators were duly appointed, and that the parties attended before them, and that an instrument purporting to be an award was made. The disputed fact is, whether the arbitrators refused wrongfully to hear any evidence on the part of the complaint ; and a point of law arises, whether, if that be so, the instrument was an award. As to the fact, the affidavits on behalf of the complainant contain sufficient to show that the justices may have been well warranted in considering it proved ; and we presume that they were right, as this is not an appeal from them. Then the point arises, did this fact warrant the statement made in the order ; in other words, does the order correctly state the legal effect of the facts ?

The 10 Geo. 4, c. 56, s. 27, enacts, that an award made according to the true purport and meaning of the rules of the society shall be final and binding. The rule of the society in question relating to arbitration, declares that the arbitrators shall hear evidence on both sides ; and their decision, binding to all parties, shall be final. Upon this statement, there is good reason for saying, that arbitrators who refused to hear the evidence of one side did not make an award according to the true meaning of the rules of this society, and therefore did not make an award final and binding within the terms and intent of the 10 Geo. 4, c. 56, s. 27.

The 4 & 5 Will. 4, c. 40, s. 7, giving jurisdiction to the justices in case of the neglect or refusal of the arbitrators to make an award, recites the 10 Geo. 4, c. 56, s. 27, and intends an award final and binding within the meaning of that statute. It seems to follow, that the justices have jurisdiction where the award is not in this sense final and binding, and we have therefore come to the conclusion that they had jurisdiction in the case now before us. Another question was, whether the justices for the county had jurisdiction, it being alleged that the matter in difference arose entirely within the jurisdiction of the borough of Leeds. But although the meetings of the society are at Leeds, and the expulsion took place there, it appears that the society is not locally confined to the borough, the members may reside out of the borough, and the act which led to the expulsion took place out of the borough, and the nature of this act was really the matter in difference. Therefore the question must be answered in the affirmative, the matter in difference not having arisen entirely within the borough of Leeds. And the rule for quashing the order of justices must be discharged.

Rule discharged.

Ex parte *Long*, 3 Weekly Reporter, 18.— *Where a dispute between a Friendly Society and one of its members has been referred to arbitration under sect. 7 of 4 & 5 Will. 4, c. 40, the award of the arbitrators is final, and a magistrate has no jurisdiction to hear the dispute, unless it can be shown that such an award is a nullity.*

C. *Hutton* moved for a rule calling on David Jardine, Esq., one of the metropolitan police magistrates, to show cause why he should not hear and determine a dispute between Amy Long, the widow of one Charles Long, and a Friendly Society, called 'The United Kingdom Benefit Society.'

It appeared by the affidavits that the husband of applicant became a member of the society in 1841, and that in October 1853, he fell ill and was declared on the sick fund of the society, and continued to receive assistance from that fund until the month of February 1854, when he received a letter from the secretary, informing him that his name was erased from the list of the members for breach of the 11th rule of the society, which was to the effect, that any member found transacting business for profit or reward, during the time he was receiving assistance from the sick fund of the society, should be excluded from the society. Charles Long died on the 25th April 1854, and the claim made by his widow, notwithstanding his expulsion, had been referred to arbitration, in accordance with the rules of the society. The arbitrators had decided against her claim, and the present application was under 4 & 5 Will. 4, c. 40, s. 7, to compel the magistrate to hear and determine the dispute.

C. *Hutton.*—It is submitted that the award of the arbitrators is bad, as having been made contrary to the rules of the society; there was no evidence of working for profit or reward. The offence charged was that during the time he was receiving aid he had wheeled a barrow for his wife, containing linen, some 400 yards. [Lord *Campbell*, C.J.—There was then some evidence; it was for the arbitrators to consider its value.] He was not summoned before the society to answer for his breach of its rules, and this objection when taken before the arbitrators was not allowed by them. — [Lord *Campbell*, C.J.—If they refused to hear the objection that the deceased had not been summoned, you might impugn the award on that refusal, but it appears they heard the objection, and refused to allow it. They did not refuse to hear the evidence on it.] That is so. [Lord *Campbell*, C.J.—It was for them to determine whether or not they would allow the objection.] The award was made corruptly; one of the arbitrators was dead. [Lord *Campbell*, C.J.—There are no facts in the affidavits to warrant that conclusion. We must suppose the arbitration to have been conducted properly. You have to show that the award was a nullity. It is not a nullity because it was against the weight of evidence. You must show that the deceased was not properly expelled—that he died a member of the society.] In *Regina* v. *Grant*, 14 Q. B. 43, an award not made according to the rules of the society was held to be void. [*Coleridge*, J.— There the award was a nullity, because the arbitrators only heard one side and refused to hear the other. Lord *Campbell*, C.J.—You must show that the award here is a nullity to give the magistrate jurisdiction to hear the case.]—He also referred to *Regina* v. *Evans*, 3 Ell. & B. 363.

Lord CAMPBELL, C.J.—I regret that no ground has been made for our interference in this case. It is a hard case, but hard cases, it is said, make bad laws. The magistrate can have no jurisdiction where the award is not a nullity. The arbitrators did not refuse to hear the evidence; they heard it, and it was for them to give what weight to it they thought right. The strongest point urged in support of the application was as to the objection having been overruled that the deceased had not been heard before expulsion. Still, the arbitrators did hear the objection, and, in spite of the objection, decided that the expulsion was regular. If *mala fides* on the part of any of the arbitrators had been satisfactorily shown, the award might have been treated as a nullity; but this charge of *mala fides* was not supported by the affidavits.

COLERIDGE, J.—I am of the same opinion. As to the argument of 'hardship,' employed in support of the application, it is one that cannot be listened to, and ought not to be put forward. Parties who become members of these societies agree that their disputes shall be settled by arbitration, and when an award is made against them they must submit to the decision. The only question in this case is, has an award been made? To give the magistrate's jurisdiction some defect, making the award a nullity, or that it has been decided with *mala fides*, must be clearly shown. Now, an award has been made, and there is not sufficient evidence of *mala fides*. We cannot listen to mere opinions as stated in the affidavits in support of such a charge. It is admitted that the objection that the deceased was not summoned was heard. The arbitrators may have decided wrongly in not giving weight to it, but still they heard it; the most that can be said is, that they came to a wrong conclusion. The case of *Regina* v. *Grant* is perfectly consistent with our decision. There one allegation was, that the arbitrators had neglected to make an award at all, that they had wrongfully refused to hear evidence, and that therefore the instrument was no award at all. The court determined, and rightly, that it was no award. That is not at all like the present case. Here the arbitrators have heard the evidence; and however mistaken they may have been in their decision, still they heard the case, and their award is valid.

WIGHTMAN, J.—The jurisdiction of the justices only arises in case the arbitrators neglect or refuse to make an award. Here they did make an award, but it is said that the arbitration was so conducted that their award is a nullity. It is said, first, that they decided wrongly; that the member expelled had not worked for profit and reward; and, secondly, that they over-ruled one of the rules of the society. As to the first objection they are to exercise their own judgment, and they have done so. As to the second, they are to determine whether the rule was infringed. They may have come to a wrong conclusion as to these points, but they have determined them to the best of their judgment. There is nothing to show *mala fides* on their parts. Their award cannot be treated as a nullity, and that is the only ground for granting this application.

ERLE, J.—I am of the same opinion. The question here is, 'Have the arbitrators made an award?' Nothing is clearer than the distinction between 'no award' and a 'mistaken award.' If persons select a mode of settling their disputes, it is important that they should be bound by it; therefore, although by coming to our present conclusion, we may inflict an apparent hardship on the party complaining, yet the effect of our decision is advantageous to these societies. The case of *Regina* v. *Grant* has been properly distinguished from the present.

Rule refused.

Reg. *v.* Rowland Evans, 3 E. & B. 363 ; 18 Justice of the Peace, 247.—*D. having been expelled by a Friendly Society, gave notice to refer the dispute to arbitration, and signed an agreement to be bound by the award of five out of nine persons, who after his expulsion had been appointed arbitrators in the room of nine others appointed at the first meeting of the society, of which nine two had become incapable of acting, and the other seven had been alleged—but this was disputed—to have left the place. The award confirmed the expulsion of D. Afterwards the society gave notice of a meeting for re-hearing D.'s case ; but D. refused to refer it again, and took out a summons before justices, who made an order for his re-admission ; Held, that the award of the arbitrators was binding, and that the order of the justices was made without jurisdiction.*

On the 12th of April 1852, David Davies was expelled from the society called the Bangor Rechabites, for an alleged breach of the rules. He disputed the lawfulness of his expulsion, and served a notice (September 8), requesting the society to refer the difference between him and the society to arbitration, as provided by the rules of the society. At the first meeting of the society, some years ago, nine arbitrators were appointed, of whom two had become incapable of acting, and the other seven were alleged in the affidavits in support of the rule to have become disqualified by quitting Bangor ; but in the affidavits against the rule, it was alleged that they were living in Bangor, and willing to act. On the 12th June 1852, nine fresh arbitrators were appointed by the society, and it did not appear that this second set of arbitrators was appointed fraudulently, or that the society had any sinister views in their appointment. The notice of Davies to refer the dispute was served on the 8th of September following. On the 6th of October, a meeting of the society was held, at which the committee and Davies attended. Six out of nine of the new arbitrators were nominated, from which the five were to be selected who were to award upon Davies's case. Davies refused to proceed with the selection, and to have his case referred, unless he was allowed to put aside one particular person of the six arbitrators. This the committee allowed him to do, and the five arbitrators were then chosen, one being an attorney, at whose suggestion an agreement in writing, simply to refer and to be bound by the award, was drawn up and signed by Davies and Rowland Evans, the president, on behalf of the society. By the rules the arbitrators were to be persons not interested in the society. Davies alleged in his affidavit that he was unaware, at the time of his referring his case, of the objection to the appointment of the second set of arbitrators, or that they had not been properly appointed. The arbitrators made their award, affirming the decision of the society as to Davies's expulsion. Then it appeared

F

that there was a notice of a meeting on February 25, 1853, to proceed to the re-hearing of Davies's case, and that the second set of arbitrators attended it, but Davies refused to refer his case to any of those persons. Davies then on the 10th March 1853, took out a summons before the justices. The hearing took place on the 15th of March, when the attorney to the society objected that the magistrates had no jurisdiction. The case was then adjourned to March 28, 1853, when five justices attended, and it was decided to hear the complaint; whereupon the attorney for the society, being dissatisfied with this decision, advised his clients to withdraw from the case, which they did: whereupon Davies proceeded to make his complaint, and the justices made an order, requiring the president of the said society forthwith to reinstate the said David Davies into the society, and adjudging that, in default of such reinstatement, the said president of the said society should forthwith after such default pay to the said David Davies the sum of 50*l*.

A rule *nisi* for quashing the order having been granted, cause was shown against the rule by *Bramwell*, Q.C., *and Willes.*

Cowling and *Hodgson, contra,* were not called on.

Lord CAMPBELL, C.J.—I am of opinion that this rule should be made absolute. The *mala fides* has been on the part of Davies. If the magistrates had decided that the appointment of the second set of arbitrators was fraudulent, they would have had jurisdiction. But they have not done so. They had no jurisdiction in this case, because there was an award made by arbitrators, whose appointment Davies had no power to contest. It would lead to the most mischievous consequences to say that the appointment of a second set of arbitrators, *bonâ fide* appointed in the belief that the Act authorized their appointment, and in the belief that the former arbitrators were dead or absent from the country, or had refused to act, could at any time afterwards be inquired into, and that, if it turned out that there had been any misapprehension, all that they had done was to become void. I am of opinion, that the second set of arbitrators was *bonâ fide* appointed, that in this case they had jurisdiction to act, and that their award was binding, and that after that Davies had no right to appeal to the justices.

COLERIDGE, J.—The question is, whether according to section 27 of the Act, and the facts in this case, the justices had jurisdiction. They had no jurisdiction unless the society had refused to comply with the application to have the dispute settled by arbitration within forty days (4 & 5 Will. 4, c. 40, s. 7), or unless there had been a neglect or refusal to make an award. When the parties were before the justices there was *de facto* an award made by the arbitrators, and there was nothing on the face to show that it was null. The burden was on Davies to show that there was no award. I agree with the argument that the award made must be a binding one on both parties. (The learned judge then recapitulated the material facts.) One of the five arbitrators chosen was an attorney, and he, supposing that all the proceedings might not be strictly regular, thought it right that an agreement should be drawn up. When these facts appear, the necessary conclusion is, that Davies was estopped from contesting the award, unless it is shown that he was deceived, and that fraud was resorted to in bringing about the award as against him. I think that this was a perfectly good award ; and it would be most mischievous if it could be re-opened under the circumstances, especially in societies of this kind.

WIGHTMAN, J.—I am of opinion that the facts and circumstances that appear on these affidavits do not warrant Davies in contesting the jurisdiction of the arbitrators.

Rule absolute.

INDEX.

MEMBER—*continued*
disputes between society, and to be settled as directed by rules, 43
by justices, 45
expelled, may be ordered to be reinstated by justices, 51
or award of arbitrators, 51
or a sum of money directed to be paid him in lieu thereof, 51
may be a witness in all proceedings respecting society, 52
minors should not be members, 15
payment of sums not exceeding 20*l.*, on death of, intestate, 40
liable for subscriptions, although funds misapplied, 7

MINORS,
should not be members, 15

MISAPPLICATION
of funds, liability for, 7

MORTGAGE,
property to be mortgaged to society, 7, 27
to be made in usual form, 7
receipt endorsed on, to vacate, 8, 29
redemption of, 18
free from stamp duty, 25
funds may be lent on, 35
forms of, 79

NATIONAL DEBT,
funds may not be invested with commissioners, 29

NEXT OF KIN,
payment to persons appearing to be, when valid, 40
remedy of, against party receiving money, 40
when money to be divided amongst, 40, 41

OFFICER,
of society, not liable for deficiency in society's funds, 40
unless he has agreed by writing to be so, 40
and deposited same with registrar, 40
amount of liability may be limited by such writing, 40
liable for money actually received, 40
or not readmitting member, 24
distress may be made upon goods of, of a society by order of justices, 44
money awarded to be paid by him, society to repay him, 45
out of first money received, 45
together with all damages incurred by him, 45
intrusted with management of funds of society to render accounts, 52
when required by order of two trustees of society, 52
or three members of committee, 52
executors and assignees of, to pay debts due to society, 52
and deliver up goods of society in their possession, 52

LONDON

PRINTED BY SPOTTISWOODE AND CO.

NEW-STREET SQUARE

GENERAL LIST OF WORKS

PUBLISHED BY

MESSRS. LONGMAN, GREEN, AND CO.

PATERNOSTER ROW, LONDON.

Historical Works.

The **HISTORY of ENGLAND** from the Fall of Wolsey to the Death of Elizabeth. By JAMES ANTHONY FROUDE, M.A. late Fellow of Exeter College, Oxford. Third Edition of the First Eight Volumes.

VOLS. I to IV. the Reign of Henry VIII. Third Edition, 54s.

VOLS. V. and VI. the Reigns of Edward VI. and Mary. Third Edition, 28s.

VOLS. VII. and VIII. the Reign of Elizabeth, VOLS. I. and II. Third Edition, 28s.

The **HISTORY of ENGLAND** from the Accession of James II. By Lord MACAULAY. Three Editions as follows.

LIBRARY EDITION, 5 vols. 8vo. £4.

CABINET EDITION, 8 vols. post 8vo. 48s.

PEOPLE'S EDITION, 4 vols. crown 8vo. 16s.

REVOLUTIONS in ENGLISH HISTORY. By ROBERT VAUGHAN, D.D. 3 vols. 8vo. 45s.

VOL. I. Revolutions of Race, 15s.

VOL II. Revolutions in Religion, 15s.

VOL. III. Revolutions in Government, 15s.

The **HISTORY of ENGLAND** during the Reign of George the Third. By WILLIAM MASSEY, M.P. 4 vols. 8vo. 48s.

The **CONSTITUTIONAL HISTORY of ENGLAND**, since the Accession of George III. 1760—1860. By THOMAS ERSKINE MAY, C.B. 2 vols. 8vo. 33s.

LIVES of the QUEENS of ENGLAND, from State Papers and other Documentary Sources : comprising a Domestic History of England from the Conquest to the Death of Queen Anne. By AGNES STRICKLAND. Revised Edition, with many Portraits. 8 vols. post 8vo. 60s.

A

LECTURES on the **HISTORY** of **ENGLAND.** By WILLIAM LONG-
MAN. VOL. I. from the earliest times to the Death of King Edward II. with
6 Maps, a coloured Plate, and 53 Woodcuts. 8vo. 15s.

A **CHRONICLE** of **ENGLAND,** from B.C. 55 to A.D. 1485 ; written
and illustrated by J. E. DOYLE. With 81 Designs engraved on Wood and
printed in Colours by E. Evans. 4to. 42s.

HISTORY of **CIVILISATION.** By HENRY THOMAS BUCKLE. 2 vols.
Price £1 17s.

> VOL. I. *England and France,* Fourth Edition, 21s.
>
> VOL. II. *Spain and Scotland,* Second Edition, 16s.

DEMOCRACY in **AMERICA.** By ALEXIS DE TOCQUEVILLE. Translated by HENRY REEVE, with an Introductory Notice by the Translator.
2 vols. 8vo. 21s.

The **SPANISH CONQUEST** in **AMERICA,** and its Relation to the
History of Slavery and to the Government of Colonies. By ARTHUR HELPS.
4 vols. 8vo. £3. VOLS. I. and II. 28s. VOLS. III. and IV. 16s. each.

HISTORY of the **REFORMATION** in **EUROPE** in the Time of
Calvin. By J. H. MERLE D'AUBIGNE, D.D. VOLS. I. and II. 8vo. 28s. and
VOL. III. 12s.

LIBRARY HISTORY of **FRANCE,** in 5 vols. 8vo. By EYRE EVANS
CROWE. VOL. I. 14s. VOL. II. 15s. VOL. III. 18s. VOL. IV. nearly ready.

LECTURES on the **HISTORY** of **FRANCE.** By the late Sir JAMES
STEPHEN, LL.D. 2 vols. 8vo. 24s.

The **HISTORY** of **GREECE.** By C. THIRLWALL, D.D., Lord Bishop
of St. David's. 8 vols. 8vo. £3; or in 8 vols. fcp. 28s.

The **TALE** of the **GREAT PERSIAN WAR,** from the Histories of
Herodotus. By the Rev. G. W. COX, M.A. late Scholar of Trin. Coll. Oxon.
Fcp. 8vo. 7s. 6d.

ANCIENT HISTORY of **EGYPT, ASSYRIA,** and **BABYLONIA.** By
the Author of 'Amy Herbert.' Fcp. 8vo. 6s.

CRITICAL HISTORY of the **LANGUAGE** and **LITERATURE** of
Ancient Greece. By WILLIAM MURE, of Caldwell. 5 vols. 8vo. £3 9s.

HISTORY of the **LITERATURE** of **ANCIENT GREECE.** By Professor K. O. MÜLLER. Translated by the Right Hon. Sir GEORGE CORNE-
WALL LEWIS, Bart. and by J. W. DONALDSON, D.D. 3 vols. 8vo. 36s.

HISTORY of the **ROMANS** under the **EMPIRE.** By the Rev.
CHARLES MERIVALE, B.D. 7 vols. 8vo. with Maps, £5.

The **FALL** of the **ROMAN REPUBLIC**: a Short History of the Last
Century of the Commonwealth. By the Rev. CHARLES MERIVALE, B.D.
12mo. 7s. 6d.

The **BIOGRAPHICAL HISTORY** of **PHILOSOPHY,** from its Origin
in Greece to the Present Day. By GEORGE HENRY LEWES. Revised and
enlarged Edition. 8vo. 16s.

HISTORY of the **INDUCTIVE SCIENCES.** By WILLIAM WHEWELL,
D.D. F.R.S. Master of Trin. Coll. Cantab. Third Edition. 3 vols. crown
8vo. 24s.

CRITICAL and HISTORICAL ESSAYS contributed to the *Edinburgh Review*. By the Right Hon. LORD MACAULAY.

    LIBRARY EDITION, 3 vols. 8vo. 36s.

    TRAVELLER'S EDITION, in 1 vol. 21s.

    In POCKET VOLUMES, 3 vols. fcp. 21s.

    PEOPLE'S EDITION, 2 vols. crown 8vo. 8s.

EGYPT'S PLACE in UNIVERSAL HISTORY; an Historical Investigation. By C. C. J. BUNSEN, D.D. Translated by C. H. COTTRELL, M.A. With many Illustrations. 4 vols. 8vo. £5 8s. VOL. V. is nearly ready.

MAUNDER'S HISTORICAL TREASURY; comprising a General Introductory Outline of Universal History, and a series of Separate Histories. Fcp. 8vo. 10s.

HISTORICAL and CHRONOLOGICAL ENCYCLOPÆDIA, presenting in a brief and convenient form Chronological Notices of all the Great Events of Universal History. By B. B. WOODWARD, F.S.A. Librarian to the Queen. [*In the press.*

HISTORY of CHRISTIAN MISSIONS; their Agents and their Results By T. W. M. MARSHALL. 2 vols. 8vo. 24s.

HISTORY of the EARLY CHURCH, from the First Preaching of the Gospel to the Council of Nicæa, A.D. 325. By the Author of 'Amy Herbert.' Fcp. 8vo. 4s. 6d.

HISTORY of WESLEYAN METHODISM. By GEORGE SMITH, F.A.S. New Edition, with Portraits, in 31 parts. Price 6d. each.

HISTORY of MODERN MUSIC; a Course of Lectures delivered at the Royal Institution. By JOHN HULLAH, Professor of Vocal Music in King's College and in Queen's College, London. Post 8vo. 6s. 6d.

HISTORY of MEDICINE, from the Earliest Ages to the Present Time. By EDWARD MERYON, M.D. F.G.S. Vol. I. 8vo. 12s. 6d.

Biography and Memoirs.

SIR JOHN ELIOT, a Biography: 1590—1632. By JOHN FORSTER. With Two Portraits on Steel from the Originals at Port Eliot. 2 vols. crown 8vo. 30s.

LETTERS and LIFE of FRANCIS BACON, including all his Occasional Works. Collected and edited, with a Commentary, by J. SPEDDING, Trin. Coll. Cantab. VOLS. I. and II. 8vo. 24s.

LIFE of ROBERT STEPHENSON, F.R.S. By J. C. JEAFFRESON, Barrister-at-Law; and WILLIAM POLE, F.R.S. Memb. Inst. Civ. Eng. With 2 Portraits and many Illustrations. 2 vols. 8vo. [*Nearly ready.*

APOLOGIA pro VITA SUA: being a Reply to a Pamphlet entitled 'What then does Dr. Newman mean?' By JOHN HENRY NEWMAN, D.D. 8vo. 14s.

LIFE of the DUKE of WELLINGTON. By the Rev. G. R. GLEIG, M.A. Popular Edition, carefully revised; with copious Additions. Crown 8vo. 5s.

Brialmont and Gleig's Life of the Duke of Wellington. 4 vols. 8vo. with Illustrations, £2 14s.

Life of the Duke of Wellington, partly from the French of M. BRIALMONT, partly from Original Documents. By the Rev. G. R. GLEIG, M.A. 8vo. with Portrait, 15s.

FATHER MATHEW: a Biography. By JOHN FRANCIS MAGUIRE, M.P. Second Edition, with Portrait. Post 8vo. 12s. 6d.

Rome; its Ruler and its Institutions. By the same Author. New Edition in preparation.

LIFE of AMELIA WILHELMINA SIEVEKING, from the German. Edited, with the Author's sanction, by CATHERINE WINKWORTH. Post 8vo. with Portrait, 12s.

FELIX MENDELSSOHN'S LETTERS from *Italy and Switzerland,* translated by LADY WALLACE, Third Edition, with Notice of MENDELSSOHN'S Life and Works, by Henry F. CHORLEY; and *Letters from 1833 to 1847,* translated by Lady WALLACE. New Edition, with Portrait. 2 vols. crown 8vo. 5s. each.

DIARIES of a LADY of QUALITY, from 1797 to 1844. Edited, with Notes, by A. Hayward, Q.C. Second Edition. Post 8vo. 10s. 6d.

RECOLLECTIONS of the late WILLIAM WILBERFORCE, M.P. for the County of York during nearly 30 Years. By J. S. HARFORD, D.C.L. F.R.S. Post 8vo. 7s.

LIFE and CORRESPONDENCE of THEODORE PARKER. By JOHN WEISS. With 2 Portraits and 19 Wood Engravings. 2 vols. 8vo. 30s.

SOUTHEY'S LIFE of WESLEY. Fifth Edition. Edited by the Rev. C. C. SOUTHEY, M.A. Crown 8vo. 7s. 6d.

THOMAS MOORE'S MEMOIRS, JOURNAL, and CORRESPONDENCE. Edited and abridged from the First Edition by Earl RUSSELL. Square crown 8vo. with 8 Portraits, 12s. 6d.

MEMOIR of the Rev. SYDNEY SMITH. By his Daughter, Lady HOLLAND. With a Selection from his Letters, edited by Mrs. AUSTIN. 2 vols. 8vo. 28s.

LIFE of WILLIAM WARBURTON, D.D. Bishop of Gloucester from 1760 to 1779. By the Rev. J. S. WATSON, M.A. 8vo. with Portrait, 18s.

FASTI EBORACENSES: Lives of the Archbishops of York. By the late Rev. W. H. DIXON, M.A. Edited and enlarged by the Rev. J. RAINE, M.A. In 2 vols. Vol. I. comprising the lives to the Death of Edward III. 8vo. 15s.

VICISSITUDES of FAMILIES. By Sir BERNARD BURKE, Ulster King of Arms. FIRST, SECOND, and THIRD SERIES. 3 vols. crown 8vo. 12s. 6d. each.

BIOGRAPHICAL SKETCHES. By NASSAU W. SENIOR. Post 8vo. price 10s. 6d.

ESSAYS in ECCLESIASTICAL BIOGRAPHY. By the Right Hon. Sir J. STEPHEN, LL.D. Fourth Edition. 8vo. 14s.

ARAGO'S BIOGRAPHIES of DISTINGUISHED SCIENTIFIC MEN. By FRANÇOIS ARAGO. Translated by Admiral W. H. SMYTH, F.R.S. the Rev. B. POWELL, M.A. and R. GRANT, M.A. 8vo. 18s.

MAUNDER'S BIOGRAPHICAL TREASURY: Memoirs, Sketches, and Brief Notices of above 12,000 Eminent Persons of All Ages and Nations. Fcp. 8vo. 10s.

Criticism, Philosophy, Polity, &c.

PAPINIAN: a Dialogue on State Affairs between a Constitutional Lawyer and a Country Gentleman about to enter Public Life. By GEORGE ATKINSON, B.A. Oxon. Serjeant-at-Law. Post 8vo. 5s.

On REPRESENTATIVE GOVERNMENT. By JOHN STUART MILL. Second Edition, 8vo. 9s.

Dissertations and Discussions. By the same Author. 2 vols. 8vo. price 24s.

On Liberty. By the same Author. Third Edition. Post 8vo. 7s. 6d.

Principles of Political Economy. By the same. Fifth Edition. 2 vols. 8vo. 30s.

A System of Logic, Ratiocinative and Inductive. By the same. Fifth Edition. Two vols. 8vo. 25s.

Utilitarianism. By the same. 8vo. 5s.

LORD BACON'S WORKS, collected and edited by R. L. ELLIS, M.A. J. SPEDDING, M.A. and D. D. HEATH. Vols. I. to V. *Philosophical Works* 5 vols. 8vo. £4 6s. VOLS. VI. and VII. *Literary and Professional Works* 2 vols. £1 16s.

BACON'S ESSAYS with ANNOTATIONS. By R. WHATELY, D.D. late Archbishop of Dublin. Sixth Edition. 8vo. 10s. 6d.

ELEMENTS of LOGIC. By R. WHATELY, D.D. late Archbishop of Dublin. Ninth Edition. 8vo. 10s. 6d. crown 8vo. 4s. 6d.

Elements of Rhetoric. By the same Author. Seventh Edition. 8vo. 10s. 6d. crown 8vo. 4s. 6d.

English Synonymes. Edited by Archbishop WHATELY. 5th Edition. Fcp. 8vo. 3s.

MISCELLANEOUS REMAINS from the Common-place Book of the late Archbishop WHATELY. Edited by Miss E. J. WHATELY. Post 8vo. 6s.

ESSAYS on the **ADMINISTRATIONS** of **GREAT BRITAIN** from 1783 to 1830, contributed to the *Edinburgh Review* by the Right Hon. Sir G. C. LEWIS, Bart. Edited by the Right Hon. Sir E. HEAD, Bart. 8vo. with Portrait, 15s.

By the same Author.

A Dialogue on the Best Form of Government, 4s. 6d.

Essay on the Origin and Formation of the Romance Languages, price 7s. 6d.

Historical Survey of the Astronomy of the Ancients, 15s.

Inquiry into the Credibility of the Early Roman History, 2 vols. price 30s.

On the Methods of Observation and Reasoning in Politics, 2 vols. price 28s.

Irish Disturbances and Irish Church Question, 12s.

Remarks on the Use and Abuse of some Political Terms, 9s.

On Foreign Jurisdiction and Extradition of Criminals, 2s. 6d.

The Fables of Babrius, Greek Text with Latin Notes, PART I. 5s. 6d. PART II. 3s. 6d.

Suggestions for the Application of the Egyptological Method to Modern History, 1s.

An **OUTLINE** of the **NECESSARY LAWS of THOUGHT**: a Treatise on Pure and Applied Logic. By the Most Rev. W. THOMSON, D.D. Archbishop of York. Crown 8vo. 5s. 6d.

The **ELEMENTS** of **LOGIC**. By THOMAS SHEDDEN, M.A. of St. Peter's Coll. Cantab. Crown 8vo. *[Just ready.*

ANALYSIS of Mr. **MILL'S SYSTEM** of **LOGIC**. By W. STEBBING, M.A. Fellow of Worcester College, Oxford. Post 8vo. *[Just ready.*

SPEECHES of the **RIGHT HON. LORD MACAULAY**, corrected by Himself. 8vo. 12s.

LORD MACAULAY'S SPEECHES on **PARLIAMENTARY REFORM** in 1831 and 1832. 16mo. 1s.

A **DICTIONARY** of the **ENGLISH LANGUAGE**. By R. G. LATHAM, M.A. M.D. F.R.S. Founded on that of Dr. JOHNSON, as edited by the Rev. H. J. TODD, with numerous Emendations and Additions. Publishing in 36 Parts, price 3s. 6d. each, to form 2 vols. 4to.

The English Language. By the same Author. Fifth Edition. 8vo. price 18s.

Handbook of the English Language. By the same Author. Fourth Edition. Crown 8vo. 7s. 6d.

Elements of Comparative Philology. By the same Author. 8vo. 21s.

THESAURUS of ENGLISH WORDS and PHRASES, classified and arranged so as to facilitate the Expression of Ideas, and assist in Literary Composition. By P. M. ROGET, M. D. 14th Edition. Crown 8vo. 10s. 6d.

LECTURES on the SCIENCE of LANGUAGE, delivered at the Royal Institution. By MAX MULLER, M.A. Fellow of All Souls College, Oxford. FIRST SERIES, Fourth Edition. 8vo. 12s. SECOND SERIES, with 31 Woodcuts, price 18s.

The **DEBATER**; a Series of Complete Debates, Outlines of Debates, and Questions for Discussion. By F. ROWTON. Fcp. 8vo. 6s.

A COURSE of ENGLISH READING, adapted to every taste and capacity; or, How and What to Read. By the Rev. J. PYCROFT, B.A. Fcp. 8vo. 5s.

MANUAL of ENGLISH LITERATURE, Historical and Critical: with a Chapter on English Metres. By T. ARNOLD, B.A. Prof. of Eng. Lit. Cath. Univ. Ireland. Post 8vo. 10s. 6d.

SOUTHEY'S DOCTOR, complete in One Volume. Edited by the Rev. J. W. WARTER, B.D. Square crown 8vo. 12s. 6d.

HISTORICAL and CRITICAL COMMENTARY on the OLD TESTAMENT; with a New Translation. By M. M. KALISCH, Ph.D. VOL. I. *Genesis*, 8vo. 18s. or adapted for the General Reader, 12s. VOL. II. *Exodus*, 15s. or adapted for the General Reader, 12s.

A Hebrew Grammar, with Exercises. By the same. PART I. *Outlines with Exercises*, 8vo. 12s. 6d. KEY, 5s. PART II. *Exceptional Forms and Constructions*, 12s. 6d.

A NEW LATIN-ENGLISH DICTIONARY. By the Rev. J. T. WHITE, M.A. of Corpus Christi College, and Rev. J. H. RIDDLE, M.A. of St. Edmund Hall, Oxford. Imperial 8vo. 42s.

A Diamond Latin-English Dictionary, or Guide to the Meaning, Quality, and Accentuation of Latin Classical Words. By the Rev. J. E. RIDDLE, M.A. 32mo. 4s.

A NEW ENGLISH-GREEK LEXICON, containing all the Greek Words used by Writers of good authority. By C. D. YONGE, B.A. Fourth Edition. 4to. 21s.

A LEXICON, ENGLISH and GREEK, abridged for the Use of Schools from his 'English-Greek Lexicon' by the Author, C. D. YONGE, B.A. Square 12mo. [*Just ready.*

A GREEK-ENGLISH LEXICON. Compiled by H. G. LIDDELL, D.D. Dean of Christ Church, and R. SCOTT, D.D. Master of Balliol. Fifth Edition. Crown 4to. 31s. 6d.

A Lexicon, Greek and English, abridged from LIDDELL and SCOTT's *Greek-English Lexicon*. Tenth Edition. Square 12mo. 7s. 6d.

A PRACTICAL DICTIONARY of the FRENCH and ENGLISH LANGUAGES. By L. CONTANSEAU. 7th Edition. Post 8vo. 10s. 6d.

Contanseau's Pocket Dictionary, French and English; being a close Abridgment of the above, by the same Author. 2nd Edition. 18mo. 5s.

NEW PRACTICAL DICTIONARY of the GERMAN LANGUAGE; German–English and English-German. By the Rev. W. L. BLACKLEY, M.A. and Dr. CARL MARTIN FRIEDLANDER. Post 8vo. [*In the press.*]

Miscellaneous Works and Popular Metaphysics.

RECREATIONS of a COUNTRY PARSON: being a Selection of the Contributions of A. K. H. B. to *Fraser's Magazine*. SECOND SERIES. Crown 8vo. 3s. 6d.

The Common-place Philosopher in Town and Country. By the same Author. Crown 8vo. 3s. 6d.

Leisure Hours in Town; Essays Consolatory, Æsthetical, Moral, Social, and Domestic. By the same. Crown 8vo. 3s. 6d.

The Autumn Holidays of a Country Parson. By the same Author. 1 vol. [*Nearly ready.*]

FRIENDS in COUNCIL: a Series of Readings and Discourses thereon. 2 vols. fcp. 8vo. 9s.

Friends in Council, SECOND SERIES. 2 vols. post 8vo. 14s.

Essays written in the Intervals of Business. Fcp. 8vo. 2s. 6d.

Companions of My Solitude. By the same Author. Fcp. 8vo. 3s. 6d.

LORD MACAULAY'S MISCELLANEOUS WRITINGS: comprising his Contributions to KNIGHT'S *Quarterly Magazine*, Articles from the Edinburgh Review not included in his *Critical and Historical Essays*, Biographies from the *Encyclopædia Britannica*, Miscellaneous Poems and Inscriptions. 2 vols. 8vo. with Portrait, 21s.

The REV. SYDNEY SMITH'S MISCELLANEOUS WORKS; including his Contributions to the *Edinburgh Review*.

    LIBRARY EDITION. 3 vols. 8vo. 36s.

    TRAVELLER'S EDITION, in 1 vol. 21s.

    In POCKET VOLUMES. 3 vols. 21s.

    PEOPLE'S EDITION. 2 vols. crown 8vo. 8s.

Elementary Sketches of Moral Philosophy, delivered at the Royal Institution. By the same Author. Fcp. 8vo. 7s.

The Wit and Wisdom of Sydney Smith: a Selection of the most memorable Passages in his Writings and Conversation. 16mo. 7s. 6d.

From MATTER to SPIRIT: the Result of Ten Years' Experience in Spirit Manifestations. By C. D. with a preface by A. B. Post 8vo. 8s. 6d.

The HISTORY of the SUPERNATURAL in All Ages and Nations, and in all Churches, Christian and Pagan; Demonstrating a Universal Faith. By WILLIAM HOWITT. 2 vols. post 8vo. 18s.

CHAPTERS on MENTAL PHYSIOLOGY. By Sir HENRY HOLLAND, Bart. M.D. F.R.S. Second Edition. Post 8vo. 8s. 6d.

ESSAYS selected from CONTRIBUTIONS to the *Edinburgh Review.* By HENRY ROGERS. Second Edition. 3 vols. fcp. 21*s.*

The Eclipse of Faith ; or, a Visit to a Religious Sceptic. By the same Author. Tenth Edition. Fcp. 8vo. 5*s.*

Defence of the Eclipse of Faith, by its Author ; a rejoinder to Dr. Newman's *Reply.* Third Edition. Fcp. 8vo. 3*s.* 6*d.*

Selections from the Correspondence of R. E. H. Greyson. By the same Author. Third Edition. Crown 8vo. 7*s.* 6*d.*

Fulleriana, or the Wisdom and Wit of THOMAS FULLER, with Essay on his Life and Genius. By the same Author. 16mo. 2*s.* 6*d.*

Reason and Faith, reprinted from the *Edinburgh Review.* By the same Author. Fourth Edition. Fcp. 8vo. 1*s.* 6*d.*

An INTRODUCTION to MENTAL PHILOSOPHY, on the Inductive Method. By. J. D. MORELL, M.A. LL.D. 8vo. 12*s.*

Elements of Psychology, containing the Analysis of the Intellectual Powers. By the same Author. Post 8vo. 7*s.* 6*d.*

The SENSES and the INTELLECT. By ALEXANDER BAIN, M.A. Professor of Logic in the University of Aberdeen. Second Edition. 8vo. price 15*s.*

The Emotions and the Will, by the same Author ; completing a Systematic Exposition of the Human Mind. 8vo. 15*s.*

On the Study of Character, including an Estimate of Phrenology. By the same Author. 8vo. 9*s.*

HOURS WITH THE MYSTICS : a Contribution to the History of Religious Opinion. By ROBERT ALFRED VAUGHAN, B.A. Second Edition. 2 vols. crown 8vo. 12*s.*

PSYCHOLOGICAL INQUIRIES, or Essays intended to illustrate the Influence of the Physical Organisation on the Mental Faculties. By Sir B. C. BRODIE, Bart. Fcp. 8vo. 5*s.* PART II. Essays intended to illustrate some Points in the Physical and Moral History of Man. Fcp. 8vo. 5*s.*

The PHILOSOPHY of NECESSITY ; or Natural Law as applicable to Mental, Moral, and Social Science. By CHARLES BRAY. Second Edition. 8vo. 9*s.*

The Education of the Feelings and Affections. By the same Author. Third Edition. 8vo. 3*s.* 6*d.*

CHRISTIANITY and COMMON SENSE. By Sir WILLOUGHBY JONES, Bart. M.A. Trin. Coll. Cantab. 8vo. 6*s.*

Astronomy, Meteorology, Popular Geography, &c.

OUTLINES of ASTRONOMY. By Sir J. F. W. HERSCHEL, Bart. M.A. Seventh Edition, revised ; with Plates and Woodcuts. 8vo. 18*s.*

ARAGO'S POPULAR ASTRONOMY. Translated by Admiral W. H. SMYTH, F.R.S. and R. GRANT, M.A. With 25 Plates and 356 Woodcuts. 2 vols. 8vo. £2 5s.

Arago's Meteorological Essays, with Introduction by Baron HUMBOLDT. Translated under the superintendence of Major-General E. SABINE, R.A. 8vo. 18s.

The **WEATHER-BOOK**; a Manual of Practical Meteorology. By Rear-Admiral ROBERT FITZ ROY, R.N. F.R.S. Third Edition, with 16 Diagrams. 8vo. 15s.

SAXBY'S WEATHER SYSTEM, or Lunar Influence on Weather, By S. M. SAXBY, R.N. Principal Instructor of Naval Engineers, H.M. Steam Reserve. Second Edition. Post 8vo. 4s.

DOVE'S LAW of STORMS considered in connexion with the ordinary Movements of the Atmosphere. Translated by R. H. SCOTT, M.A. T.C.D. 8vo. 10s. 6d.

CELESTIAL OBJECTS for **COMMON TELESCOPES.** By the Rev. T. W. WEBB, M.A. F.R.A.S. With Map of the Moon, and Woodcuts. 16mo. 7s.

PHYSICAL GEOGRAPHY for **SCHOOLS and GENERAL READERS.** By M. F. MAURY, LL.D. Author of 'Physical Geography of the Sea,' &c. Fcp. 8vo. with 2 Plates. 2s. 6d.

A DICTIONARY, Geographical, Statistical, and Historical, of the various Countries, Places, and Principal Natural Objects in the World. By J. R. M'CULLOCH, Esq. With 6 Maps. 2 vols. 8vo. 63s.

A GENERAL DICTIONARY of GEOGRAPHY, Descriptive, Physical, Statistical, and Historical: forming a complete Gazetteer of the World. By A. KEITH JOHNSTON, F.R.S.E. 8vo. 30s.

A MANUAL of GEOGRAPHY, Physical, Industrial, and Political. By W. HUGHES, F.R.G.S. Professor of Geography in King's College, and in Queen's College, London. With 6 Maps. Fcp. 8vo. 7s. 6d.

Or in Two Parts:—PART I. Europe, 3s. 6d. PART II. Asia, Africa, America, Australasia, and Polynesia, 4s.

The Geography of British History; a Geographical description of the British Islands at Successive Periods, from the Earliest Times to the Present Day. By the same. With 6 Maps. Fcp. 8vo. 8s. 6d.

The **BRITISH EMPIRE**; a Sketch of the Geography, Growth, Natural and Political Features of the United Kingdom, its Colonies and Dependencies. By CAROLINE BRAY. With 5 Maps. Fcp. 8vo. 7s. 6d.

COLONISATION and **COLONIES**: a Series of Lectures delivered before the University of Oxford. By HERMAN MERIVALE, M.A. Professor of Political Economy. 8vo. 18s.

The **AFRICANS** at **HOME**: a popular Description of Africa and the Africans. By the Rev. R. M. MACBRAIR, M.A. Second Edition; including an Account of the Discovery of the Source of the Nile. With Map and 70 Woodcuts. Fcp. 8vo. 5s.

MAUNDER'S TREASURY of GEOGRAPHY, Physical, Historical, Descriptive, and Political. Completed by W. HUGHES, F.R.G.S. With 7 Maps and 16 Plates. Fcp. 8vo. 10s.

Natural History and Popular Science.

The **ELEMENTS** of **PHYSICS** or **NATURAL PHILOSOPHY**. By NEIL ARNOTT, M.D. F.R.S. Physician Extraordinary to the Queen. Sixth Edition. PART I. 8vo. 10s. 6d.

HEAT CONSIDERED as a **MODE** of **MOTION**; a Course of Lecture. delivered at the Royal Institution. By Professor JOHN TYNDALL, F.R.S. Crown 8vo. with Woodcuts, 12s. 6d.

VOLCANOS, the Character of their Phenomena, their Share in the Structure and Composition of the Surface of the Globe, &c. By G. POULETT SCROPE, M.P. F.R.S. Second Edition. 8vo. with illustrations, 15s.

A **TREATISE** on **ELECTRICITY**, in Theory and Practice. By A. DE LA RIVE, Prof. in the Academy of Geneva. Translated by C. V. WALKER, F.R.S. 3 vols. 8vo. with Woodcuts, £3 13s.

The **CORRELATION** of **PHYSICAL FORCES**. By W. R. GROVE, Q.C. V.P.R.S. Fourth Edition. 8vo. 7s. 6d.

The **GEOLOGICAL MAGAZINE**; or, Monthly Journal of Geology Edited by T. RUPERT JONES, F.G.S. Professor of Geology in the R. M. College, Sandhurst; assisted by J. C. WOODWARD, F.G.S. F.Z.S. British Museum. 8vo. with Illustrations, price 1s. 6d. monthly.

A **GUIDE** to **GEOLOGY**. By J. PHILLIPS, M.A. Professor of Geology in the University of Oxford. Fifth Edition; with Plates and Diagrams. Fcp. 8vo. 4s.

A **GLOSSARY** of **MINERALOGY**. By H. W. BRISTOW, F.G.S. of the Geological Survey of Great Britain. With 486 Figures. Crown 8vo. 12s.

PHILLIPS'S ELEMENTARY INTRODUCTION to **MINERALOGY**, with extensive Alterations and Additions, by H. J. BROOKE, F.R.S. and W. H. MILLER, F.G.S. Post 8vo. with Woodcuts, 18s.

VAN DER HOEVEN'S HANDBOOK of **ZOOLOGY**. Translated from the Second Dutch Edition by the Rev. W. CLARK, M.D. F.R.S. 2 vols. 8vo. with 24 Plates of Figures, 60s.

The **COMPARATIVE ANATOMY** and **PHYSIOLOGY** of the **VERTE**brate Animals. By RICHARD OWEN, F.R.S. D.C.L. 2 vols. 8vo. with upwards of 1,200 Woodcuts. [In the press.

HOMES WITHOUT HANDS: an Account of the Habitations constructed by various Animals, classed according to their Principles of Construction. By Rev. J. G. WOOD, M.A. F.L.S. Illustrations on Wood by G. Pearson, from Drawings by F. W. Keyl and E. A. Smith. In course of publication in 20 Parts, 1s. each.

MANUAL of CŒLENTERATA. By J. REAY GREENE, B.A. M.R.I.A. Edited by the Rev. J. A. GALBRAITH, M.A. and the Rev. S. HAUGHTON, M.D. Fcp. 8vo. with 39 Woodcuts. 5s.

Manual of Protozoa: with a General Introduction on the Principles of Zoology. By the same Author and Editors. Fcp. 8vo. with 16 Woodcuts, 2s.

Manual of the Metalloids. By J. APJOHN, M.D. F.R.S. and th same Editors. Fcp. 8vo. with 38 Woodcuts, 7s. 6d.

THE ALPS: Sketches of Life and Nature in the Mountains. By Baron H. VON BERLEPSCH. Translated by the Rev. L. STEPHEN, M.A. With 17 Illustrations. 8vo. 15s.

The SEA and its LIVING WONDERS. By Dr. G. HARTWIG. Second (English) Edition. 8vo. with many Illustrations. 18s.

The TROPICAL WORLD. By the same Author. With 8 Chromo-xylographs and 172 Woodcuts. 8vo. 21s.

SKETCHES of the NATURAL HISTORY of CEYLON. By Sir J. EMERSON TENNENT, K.C.S. LL.D. With 82 Wood Engravings. Post 8vo. price 12s. 6d.

Ceylon. By the same Author. 5th Edition ; with Maps, &c. and 90 Wood Engravings. 2 vols. 8vo. £2 10s.

MARVELS and MYSTERIES of INSTINCT; or, Curiosities of Animal Life. By G. GARRATT. Third Edition. Fcp. 8vo. 7s.

HOME WALKS and HOLIDAY RAMBLES. By the Rev. C. A. JOHNS, B.A. F.L.S. Fcp. 8vo. with 10 Illustrations, 6s.

KIRBY and SPENCE'S INTRODUCTION to ENTOMOLOGY, or Elements of the Natural History of Insects. Seventh Edition. Crown 8vo. price 5s.

MAUNDER'S TREASURY of NATURAL HISTORY, or Popular Dictionary of Zoology. Revised and corrected by T. S. COBBOLD. M.D, Fcp. 8vo. with 900 Woodcuts, 10s.

The TREASURY of BOTANY, on the Plan of Maunder's Treasury. By J. LINDLEY, M.D. and T. MOORE, F.L.S. assisted by other Practical Botanists. With 16 Plates, and many Woodcuts from designs by W. H. Fitch. Fcp. 8vo.   [In the press.

The ROSE AMATEUR'S GUIDE. By THOMAS RIVERS. 8th Edition. Fcp. 8vo. 4s.

The BRITISH FLORA; comprising the Phænogamous or Flowering Plants and the Ferns. By Sir W. J. HOOKER, K.H. and G. A. WALKER ARNOTT, LL.D. 12mo. with 12 Plates, 14s. or coloured, 21s.

BRYOLOGIA BRITANNICA; containing the Mosses of Great Britain and Ireland, arranged and described. By W. WILSON. 8vo. with 61 Plates 42s. or coloured, £4 4s.

The INDOOR GARDENER. By Miss MALING. Fcp. 8vo. with coloured Frontispiece, 5s.

LOUDON'S ENCYCLOPÆDIA of PLANTS; comprising the Specific Character, Description, Culture, History, &c. of all the Plants found in Great Britain. With upwards of 12,000 Woodcuts. 8vo. £3 13s. 6d.

Loudon's Encyclopædia of Trees and Shrubs; containing the Hardy Trees and Shrubs of Great Britain scientifically and popularly described. With 2,000 Woodcuts. 8vo. 50s.

HISTORY of the BRITISH FRESHWATER ALGÆ. By A. H. HASSALL, M.D. With 100 Plates of Figures. 2 vols. 8vo. price £1 15s.

MAUNDER'S SCIENTIFIC and LITERARY TREASURY; a Popular Encyclopædia of Science, Literature, and Art.   Fcp. 8vo. 10s.

A DICTIONARY of SCIENCE, LITERATURE and ART; comprising the History, Description, and Scientific Principles of every Branch of Human Knowledge. Edited by W. T. BRANDE, F.R.S.L. and E. Fourth Edition, revised and corrected.   [In the press.

ESSAYS on SCIENTIFIC and other SUBJECTS, contributed to the Edinburgh and Quarterly Reviews.   By Sir H. HOLLAND, Bart. M.D. Second Edition. 8vo. 14s.

ESSAYS from the EDINBURGH and QUARTERLY REVIEWS; with Addresses and other pieces. By Sir J. F. W. HERSCHEL, Bart, M.A. 8vo. 18s.

Chemistry, Medicine, Surgery, and the Allied Sciences.

A DICTIONARY of CHEMISTRY and the Allied Branches of other Sciences; founded on that of the late Dr. Ure. By HENRY WATTS, F.C.S. assisted by eminent Contributors. 4 vols. 8vo. in course of publication in Monthly Parts. VOL. I. 31s. 6d. and VOL. 11. 26s. are now ready.

HANDBOOK of CHEMICAL ANALYSIS, adapted to the Unitary System of Notation: Based on Dr. H. Wills' Anleitung zur chemischen Analyse. By F. T. CONINGTON, M.A. F.C.S.   Post 8vo. 7s. 6d.—TABLES of QUALITATIVE ANALYSIS to accompany the same, 2s. 6d.

A HANDBOOK of VOLUMETRICAL ANALYSIS.   By ROBERT H. SCOTT, M.A. T.C.D. Post 8vo. 4s. 6d.

ELEMENTS of CHEMISTRY, Theoretical and Practical.   By WILLIAM A. MILLER, M.D. LL.D. F.R.S. F.G.S. Professor of Chemistry, King's College, London. 3 vols. 8vo. £2 12s.   PART I.   CHEMICAL PHYSICS. Third Edition enlarged, 12s. PART II. INORGANIC CHEMISTRY. Second Edition, 20s. PART III. ORGANIC CHEMISTRY. Second Edition, 20s.

A MANUAL of CHEMISTRY, Descriptive and Theoretical.   By WILLIAM ODLING, M.B. F.R.S. Lecturer on Chemistry at St. Bartholomew's Hospital. PART I. 8vo. 9s.

A Course of Practical Chemistry, for the use of Medical Students. By the same Author. PART I. crown 8vo. with Woodcuts, 4s. 6d. PART II. (completion) just ready.

The DIAGNOSIS and TREATMENT of the DISEASES of WOMEN; including the Diagnosis of Pregnancy. By GRAILY HEWITT, M.D. Physician to the British Lying-in Hospital. 8vo. 16s.

LECTURES on the DISEASES of INFANCY and CHILDHOOD. By CHARLES WEST, M.D. &c. Fourth Edition, revised and enlarged. 8vo. 14s.

EXPOSITION of the SIGNS and SYMPTOMS of PREGNANCY; with other Papers on subjects connected with Midwifery.   By W. MONTGOMERY, M.A. M.D. M.R.I.A. 8vo. with Illustrations, 25s.

A **SYSTEM of SURGERY**, Theoretical and Practical. In Treatises by Various Authors, arranged and edited by T. HOLMES, M.A. Cantab. Assistant-Surgeon to St. George's Hospital. 4 vols. 8vo.

Vol. I. **General Pathology.** 21s.

Vol. II. **Local Injuries—Diseases of the Eye.** 21s.

Vol. III. **Operative Surgery. Diseases of the Organs of Special** Sense, Respiration, Circulation, Locomotion and Innervation. 21s.

Vol. IV. **Diseases of the Alimentary Canal, of the Urine-genitary** Organs, of the Thyroid, Mamma and Skin; with Appendix of Miscellaneous Subjects, and GENERAL INDEX. *[Early in October.*

LECTURES on the **PRINCIPLES** and **PRACTICE** of **PHYSIC.** By THOMAS WATSON, M.D. Physician-Extraordinary to the Queen. Fourth Edition. 2 vols. 8vo. 34s.

LECTURES on **SURGICAL PATHOLOGY.** By J. PAGET, F.R.S. Surgeon-Extraordinary to the Queen. Edited by W. TURNER, M.B. 8vo. with 117 Woodcuts, 21s.

A **TREATISE** on the **CONTINUED FEVERS of GREAT BRITAIN.** By C. MURCHISON, M.D. Senior Physician to the London Fever Hospital. 8vo. with coloured Plates, 18s.

DEMONSTRATIONS of MICROSCOPIC ANATOMY; a Guide to the Examination of the Animal Tissues and Fluids in Health and Disease, for the use of the Medical and Veterinary Professions. Founded on a Course of Lectures delivered by Dr. HARLEY, Prof. in Univ. Coll. London. Edited by G. T. BROWN, late Vet. Prof. in the Royal Agric. Coll. Cirencester. 8vo. with Illustrations. *[Nearly ready.*

ANATOMY, DESCRIPTIVE and SURGICAL. By HENRY GRAY, F.R.S. With 410 Wood Engravings from Dissections. Third Edition, by T. HOLMES, M.A. Cantab. Royal 8vo. 28s.

PHYSIOLOGICAL ANATOMY and PHYSIOLOGY of MAN. By the late R. B. TODD, M.D. F.R.S. and W. BOWMAN, F.R.S. of King's College. With numerous Illustrations. VOL. II. 8vo. 25s.

A **New Edition of the FIRST VOLUME,** by Dr. LIONEL S. BEALE, is preparing for publication.

The **CYCLOPÆDIA of ANATOMY and PHYSIOLOGY.** Edited by the late R. B. TODD, M.D. F.R.S. Assisted by nearly all the most eminent cultivators of Physiological Science of the present age. 5 vols. 8vo. with 2,853 Woodcuts, £6 6s.

A **DICTIONARY of PRACTICAL MEDICINE.** By J. COPLAND, M.D. F.R.S. Abridged from the larger work by the Author, assisted by J. C. COPLAND. 1 vol. 8vo. *[In the press.*

Dr. **Copland's Dictionary of Practical Medicine** (the larger work). 3 vols. 8vo. £5 11s.

The **WORKS of SIR B. C. BRODIE,** Bart. Edited by CHARLES HAWKINS, F.R.C.S.E. 2 vols. 8vo. *[In the press.*

MEDICAL NOTES and REFLECTIONS. By Sir H. HOLLAND, Bart. M.D. Third Edition. 8vo. 18s.

HOOPER'S MEDICAL DICTIONARY, or Encyclopædia of Medical Science. Ninth Edition, brought down to the present time, by ALEX. HENRY, M.D. 1 vol. 8vo.   [*In the press.*

A MANUAL of MATERIA MEDICA and THERAPEUTICS, abridged from Dr. PEREIRA's *Elements* by F. J. FARRE, M.D. Cantab. assisted by R. BENTLEY, M.R.C.S. and by R. WARRINGTON, F.C.S. 1 vol. 8vo.

Dr. Pereira's Elements of Materia Medica and Therapeutics, Third Edition. By A. S. TAYLOR, M.D. and G. O. REES, M.D. 3 vols. 8vo. with numerous Woodcuts, £3 15s.

The Fine Arts, and Illustrated Editions.

The NEW TESTAMENT of OUR LORD and SAVIOUR JESUS CHRIST. Illustrated with numerous Engravings on Wood from the OLD MASTERS. Crown 4to. price 63s. cloth, gilt top; or price £5 5s. elegantly bound in morocco.   [*In October.*

LYRA GERMANICA; Hymns for the Sundays and Chief Festivals of the Christian Year. Translated by CATHERINE WINKWORTH: 125 Illustrations on Wood drawn by J. LEIGHTON, F.S.A. Fcp. 4to. 21s.

CATS' and FARLIE'S MORAL EMBLEMS; with Aphorisms, Adages, and Proverbs of all Nations: comprising 121 Illustrations on Wood by J. LEIGHTON, F.S.A. with an appropriate Text by R. PIGOTT. Imperial 8vo. 31s. 6d.

BUNYAN'S PILGRIM'S PROGRESS: with 126 Illustrations on Steel and Wood by C. BENNETT; and a Preface by the Rev. C. KINGSLEY. Fcp. 4to. 21s.

The HISTORY of OUR LORD, as exemplified in Works of Art: with that of His Types, St. John the Baptist, and other Persons of the Old and New Testament. By Mrs. JAMESON and Lady EASTLAKE. Being the Fourth and concluding SERIES of 'Sacred and Legendary Art;' with 31 Etchings and 281 Woodcuts. 2 vols. square crown 8vo. 42s.

In the same Series, by Mrs. JAMESON.

Legends of the Saints and Martyrs. Fourth Edition, with 19 Etchings and 187 Woodcuts. 2 vols. 31s. 6d.

Legends of the Monastic Orders. Third Edition, with 11 Etchings and 88 Woodcuts. 1 vol. 21s.

Legends of the Madonna. Third Edition, with 27 Etchings and 165 Woodcuts. 1 vol. 21s.

Arts, Manufactures, &c.

ENCYCLOPÆDIA of ARCHITECTURE, Historical, Theoretical, and Practical. By JOSEPH GWILT. With more than 1,000 Woodcuts. 8vo. 42s.

TUSCAN SCULPTORS, their Lives, Works, and Times. With Illustrations from Original Drawings and Photographs. By CHARLES C. PERKINS. 2 vols. imperial 8vo. *[In the press.*

The **ENGINEER'S HANDBOOK**; explaining the Principles which should guide the young Engineer in the Construction of Machinery. By C. S. LOWNDES. Post 8vo. 5s.

The **ELEMENTS of MECHANISM**, for Students of Applied Mechanics. By T. M. GOODEVE, M.A. Professor of Nat. Philos. in King's Coll. London. With 206 Woodcuts. Post 8vo. 6s. 6d.

URE'S DICTIONARY of ARTS, MANUFACTURES, and MINES. Re-written and enlarged by ROBERT HUNT, F.R.S. assisted by numerous gentlemen eminent in Science and the Arts. With 2,000 Woodcuts. 3 vols. 8vo. £4.

ENCYCLOPÆDIA of CIVIL ENGINEERING, Historical, Theoretical, and Practical. By E. CRESY, C.E. With above 3,000 Woodcuts. 8vo. 42s.

TREATISE on MILLS and MILLWORK. By W. FAIRBAIRN, C.E. F.R.S. With 18 Plates and 322 Woodcuts. 2 vols. 8vo. 32s. or each vol. separately, 16s.

Useful Information for Engineers. By the same Author. FIRST and SECOND SERIES, with many Plates and Woodcuts. 2 vols. crown 8vo. 21s. or each vol. separately, 10s. 6d.

The **Application of Cast and Wrought Iron to Building Purposes.** By the same Author. Third Edition, with Plates and Woodcuts. *[Nearly ready.*

The **PRACTICAL MECHANIC'S JOURNAL**: An Illustrated Record of Mechanical and Engineering Science, and Epitome of Patent Inventions. 4to. price 1s. monthly.

The **PRACTICAL DRAUGHTSMAN'S BOOK of INDUSTRIAL DESIGN.** By W. JOHNSON, Assoc. Inst. C.E. With many hundred Illustrations. 4to. 28s. 6d.

The **PATENTEE'S MANUAL**; a Treatise on the Law and Practice of Letters Patent for the use of Patentees and Inventors. By J. and J. H. JOHNSON. Post 8vo. 7s. 6d.

The **ARTISAN CLUB'S TREATISE on the STEAM ENGINE**, in its various Applications to Mines, Mills, Steam Navigation, Railways and Agriculture. By J. BOURNE, C.E. Fifth Edition; with 37 Plates and 546 Woodcuts. 4to. 42s.

A Catechism of the Steam Engine, in its various Applications to Mines, Mills, Steam Navigation, Railways, and Agriculture. By the same Author. With 80 Woodcuts. Fcp. 8vo. 6s.

The **STORY of the GUNS.** By Sir J. EMERSON TENNENT, K.C.S. F.R.S. With 33 Woodcuts. Post 8vo. 7s. 6d.

The **THEORY of WAR** Illustrated by numerous Examples from History. By Lieut.-Col. P. L. MACDOUGALL. *Third Edition*, with 10 Plans. Post 8vo. 10s. 6d.

COLLIERIES and COLLIERS; A Handbook of the Law and leading. Cases relating thereto. By J. C. FOWLER, Barrister-at-Law. Fcp. 8vo. 6s.

The ART of PERFUMERY; the History and Theory of Odours, and the Methods of Extracting the Aromas of Plants. By Dr. PIESSE, F.C.S. Third Edition, with 53 Woodcuts. Crown 8vo. 10s. 6d.

Chemical, Natural, and Physical Magic, for Juveniles during the Holidays. By the same Author. With 30 Woodcuts. Fcp. 8vo. 3s. 6d.

The Laboratory of Chemical Wonders: a Scientific Mélange for Young People. By the same. Crown 8vo. 5s. 6d.

TALPA; or the Chronicles of a Clay Farm. By C. W. HOSKYNS, Esq. With 24 Woodcuts from Designs by G. CRUIKSHANK. 16mo. 5s. 6d.

H.R.H. the PRINCE CONSORT'S FARMS: An Agricultural Memoir. By JOHN CHALMERS MORTON. Dedicated by permission to Her Majesty the QUEEN. With 40 Wood Engravings. 4to. 52s. 6d.

Handbook of Farm Labour, Steam, Water, Wind, Horse Power, Hand Power, &c. By the same Author. 16mo. 1s. 6d.

Handbook of Dairy Husbandry; comprising the General Management of a Dairy Farm, &c. By the same. 16mo. 1s. 6d.

LOUDON'S ENCYCLOPÆDIA of AGRICULTURE: comprising the Laying-out, Improvement, and Management of Landed Property, and the Cultivation and Economy of the Productions of Agriculture. With 1,100 Woodcuts. 8vo. 31s. 6d.

Loudon's Encylopædia of Gardening: Comprising the Theory and Practice of Horticulture, Floriculture, Arboriculture, and Landscape Gardening. With 1,000 Woodcuts. 8vo. 31s. 6d.

Loudon's Encyclopædia of Cottage, Farm, and Villa Architecture and Furniture. With more than 2,000 Woodcuts. 8vo. 42s.

HISTORY of WINDSOR GREAT PARK and WINDSOR FOREST. By WILLIAM MENZIES, Resident Deputy Surveyor. Dedicated by permission to H. M. the QUEEN. With 2 Maps, and 20 Photographs by the EARL of CAITHNESS and Mr. BEMBRIDGE. Imperial folio, £8 8s.

BAYLDON'S ART of VALUING RENTS and TILLAGES, and Claims of Tenants upon Quitting Farms, both at Michaelmas and Lady-Day. Eighth Edition, adapted to the present time by J. C. MORTON.

Religious and Moral Works.

An **EXPOSITION of the 39 ARTICLES,** Historical and Doctrinal. By E. HAROLD BROWNE, D.D. Lord Bishop of Ely. Sixth Edition, 8vo. 16s.

The Pentateuch and the Elohistic Psalms, in reply to Bishop Colenso. By the same Author. 8vo. 2s.

Examination Questions on Bishop Browne's Exposition of the Articles. By the Rev. J. GORLE, M.A. Fcp. 3s. 6d.

FIVE LECTURES on the CHARACTER of ST. PAUL; being the Hulsean Lectures for 1862. By the Rev. J. S. Howson, D.D. Second Edition. 8vo. 9s.

A CRITICAL and GRAMMATICAL COMMENTARY on ST. PAUL'S Epistles. By C. J. Ellicott, D.D. Lord Bishop of Gloucester and Bristol. 8vo.

Galatians, Third Edition, 8s. 6d.

Ephesians, Third Edition, 8s. 6d.

Pastoral Epistles, Second Edition, 10s. 6d.

Philippians, Colossians, and Philemon, Second Edition, 10s. 6d.

Thessalonians, Second Edition, 7s. 6d.

Historical Lectures on the Life of our Lord Jesus Christ: being the Hulsean Lectures for 1859. By the same. Third Edition. 8vo. 10s. 6d.

The Destiny of the Creature; and other Sermons preached before the University of Cambridge. By the same. Post 8vo. 5s.

The Broad and the Narrow Way; Two Sermons preached before the University of Cambridge. By the same. Crown 8vo. 2s.

Rev. T. H. HORNE'S INTRODUCTION to the CRITICAL STUDY and Knowledge of the Holy Scriptures. Eleventh Edition, corrected and extended under careful Editorial revision. With 4 Maps and 22 Woodcuts and Facsimiles. 4 vols. 8vo. £3 13s. 6d.

Rev. T. H. Horne's Compendious Introduction to the Study of the Bible, being an Analysis of the larger work by the same Author. Re-edited by the Rev. John Ayre, M.A. With Maps. &c. Post 8vo. 9s.

The TREASURY of BIBLE KNOWLEDGE, on the Plan of Maunder's Treasuries. By the Rev. John Ayre, M.A. Fcp. 8vo. with Maps and Illustrations. [In the press.

The GREEK TESTAMENT; with Notes, Grammatical and Exegetical. By the Rev. W. Webster, M.A. and the Rev. W. F. Wilkinson, M.A. 2 vols. 8vo. £2 4s.

> Vol. I. the Gospels and Acts, 20s.
> Vol. II. the Epistles and Apocalypse, 24s.

The FOUR EXPERIMENTS in Church and State; and the Conflicts of Churches. By Lord Robert Montagu, M.P. 8vo. 12s.

EVERY-DAY SCRIPTURE DIFFICULTIES explained and illustrated; Gospels of St. Matthew and St. Mark. By J. E. Prescott, M.A. late Fellow of C. C. Coll. Cantab. 8vo. 9s.

The PENTATEUCH and BOOK of JOSHUA Critically Examined. By J. W. Colenso, D.D. Lord Bishop of Natal. Part I. *the Pentateuch examined as an Historical Narrative.* 8vo. 6s. Part II. *the Age and Authorship of the Pentateuch Considered,* 7s. 6d. Part III. *the Book of Deuteronomy,* 8s. Part IV. *the First 11 Chapters of Genesis examined and separated, with Remarks on the Creation, the Fall, and the Deluge,* 10s. 6d.

The **LIFE** and **EPISTLES** of **ST. PAUL**. By W. J. CONYBEARE, M.A. late Fellow of Trin. Coll. Cantab. and J. S. HOWSON, D.D. Principal of the Collegiate Institution, Liverpool.

LIBRARY EDITION, with all the Original Illustrations, Maps, Landscapes on Steel, Woodcuts, &c.   2 vols. 4to. 48s.

INTERMEDIATE EDITION, with a Selection of Maps, Plates, and Woodcuts. 2 vols. square crown 8vo. 31s. 6d.

PEOPLE'S EDITION, revised and condensed, with 46 Illustrations and Maps.   2 vols. crown 8vo. 12s.

The **VOYAGE** and **SHIPWRECK** of **ST. PAUL**; with Dissertations on the Ships and Navigation of the Ancients.   By JAMES SMITH, F.R.S. Crown 8vo. Charts, 8s. 6d.

HIPPOLYTUS and his **AGE**; or, the Beginnings and Prospects of Christianity.   By Baron BUNSEN, D.D.   2 vols. 8vo. 30s.

Outlines of the Philosophy of Universal History, applied to Language and Religion : Containing an Account of the Alphabetical Conferences. By the same Author.   2 vols. 8vo. 33s.

Analecta Ante-Nicæna.   By the same Author.   3 vols. 8vo. 42s.

THEOLOGIA GERMANICA.   Translated by SUSANNAH WINKWORTH: with a Preface by the Rev. C. KINGSLEY ; and a Letter by Baron BUNSEN. Fcp. 8vo. 5s.

INSTRUCTIONS in the **DOCTRINE** and **PRACTICE** of **CHRIS-**tianity, as an Introduction to Confirmation.   By G. E. L. COTTON, D.D. Lord Bishop of Calcutta. 18mo. 2s. 6d.

ESSAYS on **RELIGION** and **LITERATURE**.   By Cardinal WISEMAN, Dr. D. ROCK, F. H. LAING, and other Writers.   Edited by H. E. MANNING, D.D.   8vo.

ESSAYS and **REVIEWS.**   By the Rev. W. TEMPLE, D.D. the Rev. R. WILLIAMS, B.D. the Rev. B. POWELL, M.A. the Rev. H. B. WILSON, B.D. C. W. GOODWIN, M.A. the Rev. M. PATTISON, B.D. and the Rev. B. JOWETT, M.A. 11th Edition.   Fcp. 8vo. 5s.

MOSHEIM'S ECCLESIASTICAL HISTORY.   MURDOCK and SOAMES'S Translation and Notes, re-edited by the Rev. W. STUBBS, M.A.   3 vols. 8vo. 45s.

The **GENTILE** and the **JEW** in the Courts of the Temple of Christ : an Introduction to the History of Christianity.   From the German of Prof. DÖLLINGER, by the Rev. N. DARNELL, M.A.   2 vols. 8vo. 21s.

PHYSICO-PROPHETICAL ESSAYS, on the Locality of the Eternal Inheritance, its Nature and Character ; the Resurrection Body ; and the Mutual Recognition of Glorified Saints.   By the Rev. W. LISTER, F.G.S. Crown 8vo. 6s.

BISHOP JEREMY TAYLOR'S ENTIRE WORKS: With Life by BISHOP HEBER.   Revised and corrected by the Rev. C. P. EDEN, 10 vols. 8vo. £5 5s.

PASSING THOUGHTS on RELIGION. By the Author of 'Amy Herbert.' 8th Edition. Fcp. 8vo. 5s.

Thoughts for the Holy Week, for Young Persons. By the same Author. 2d Edition. Fcp. 8vo. 2s.

Night Lessons from Scripture. By the same Author. 2d Edition. 32mo. 3s.

Self-Examination before Confirmation. By the same Author. 32mo. price 1s. 6d.

Readings for a Month Preparatory to Confirmation, from Writers of the Early and English Church. By the same. Fcp. 4s.

Readings for Every Day in Lent, compiled from the Writings of Bishop JEREMY TAYLOR. By the same. Fcp. 8vo. 5s.

Preparation for the Holy Communion; the Devotions chiefly from the works of JEREMY TAYLOR. By the same. 32mo. 3s.

MORNING CLOUDS. Second Edition. Fcp. 8vo. 5s.

The Afternoon of Life. By the same Author. Second Edition. Fcp. 5s.

Problems in Human Nature. By the same. Post 8vo. 5s.

The WIFE'S MANUAL; or, Prayers, Thoughts, and Songs on Several Occasions of a Matron's Life. By the Rev. W. CALVERT, M.A. Crown 8vo. price 10s. 6d.

SPIRITUAL SONGS for the SUNDAYS and HOLIDAYS throughout the Year. By J. S. B. MONSELL, LL.D. Vicar of Egham. Third Edition. Fcp. 8vo. 4s. 6d.

HYMNOLOGIA CHRISTIANA: or, Psalms and Hymns selected and arranged in the order of the Christian Seasons. By B. H. KENNEDY, D.D. Prebendary of Lichfield. Crown 8vo. 7s. 6d.

LYRA SACRA; Hymns, Ancient and Modern, Odes and Fragments of Sacred Poetry. Edited by the Rev. B. W. SAVILE, M.A. Fcp. 8vo. 5s.

LYRA GERMANICA, translated from the German by Miss C. WINKWORTH. FIRST SERIES, Hymns for the Sundays and Chief Festivals; SECOND SERIES, the Christian Life. Fcp. 8vo. 5s. each SERIES.

Hymns from Lyra Germanica, 18mo. 1s.

LYRA EUCHARISTICA; Hymns and Verses on the Holy Communion, Ancient and Modern: with other Poems. Edited by the Rev. ORBY SHIPLEY, M.A. Second Edition, revised and enlarged. Fcp. 8vo. 7s. 6d.

Lyra Messianica; Hymns and Verses on the Life of Christ, Ancient and Modern; with other Poems. By the same Editor. Fcp. 8vo. 7s. 6d.

Lyra Mystica; Hymns and Verses on Sacred Subjects, Ancient and Modern. Forming a companion volume to the above, by the same Editor. Fcp. 8vo.   [*Nearly ready.*]

LYRA DOMESTICA; Christian Songs for Domestic Edification. Translated from the *Psaltery and Harp* of C. J. P. SPITTA, and from other sources, by RICHARD MASSIE. FIRST and SECOND SERIES, fcp. 8vo. price 4*s.* 6*d.* each.

The **CHORALE BOOK** for **ENGLAND**; a complete Hymn-Book in accordance with the Services and Festivals of the Church of England: the Hymns translated by Miss C. WINKWORTH; the tunes arranged by Prof. W. S. BENNETT and OTTO GOLDSCHMIDT. Fcp. 4to. 10*s.* 6*d.*

Congregational Edition. Fcp. 8vo. price 1*s.* 6*d.*

Travels, Voyages, &c.

EASTERN EUROPE and **WESTERN ASIA.** Political and Social Sketches on Russia, Greece, and Syria. By HENRY A. TILLEY. With 6 Illustrations. Post 8vo. 10*s.* 6*d.*

EXPLORATIONS in **SOUTH-WEST AFRICA**, from Walvisch Bay to Lake Ngami and the Victoria Falls. By THOMAS BAINES. 8vo. with Map and Illustrations.　　　　　　　　　　　　　　　　 [*In October.*

SOUTH AMERICAN SKETCHES; or, a Visit to Rio Janeiro, the Organ Mountains, La Plata, and the Paraná. By THOMAS W. HINCHLIFF, M.A. F.R.G.S. Post 8vo. with Illustrations, 12*s.* 6*d.*

EXPLORATIONS in **LABRADOR.** By HENRY Y. HIND, M.A. F.R.G.S. With Maps and Illustrations. 2 vols. 8vo. 32*s.*

The **Canadian Red River** and **Assinniboine** and **Saskatchewan** Exploring Expeditions. By the same Author. With Maps and Illustrations. 2 vols. 8vo. 42*s.*

The **CAPITAL of the TYCOON**; a Narrative of a Three Years' Residence in Japan. By Sir RUTHERFORD ALCOCK, K.C.B. 2 vols. 8vo. with numerous Illustrations, 42*s.*

LAST WINTER in **ROME** and other **ITALIAN CITIES.** By C. R. WELD, Author of 'The Pyrenees, West and East,' &c. 1 vol. post 8vo. with a Portrait of 'STELLA,' and Engravings on Wood from Sketches by the Author.　　　　　　　　　　　　　　　　　　 [*In the Autumn.*

AUTUMN RAMBLES in **NORTH AFRICA.** By JOHN ORMSBY, of the Middle Temple, Author of the 'Ascent of the Grivola,' in 'Peaks, Passes, and Glaciers.' With 13 Illustrations on Wood from Sketches by the Author. Post 8vo. 8*s.* 6*d.*

PEAKS, PASSES, and **GLACIERS**; a Series of Excursions by Members of the Alpine Club. Edited by J. BALL, M.R.I.A. Fourth Edition; Maps, Illustrations, Woodcuts. Square crown 8vo. 21*s.*—TRAVELLERS' EDITION, condensed, 16mo. 5*s.* 6*d.*

Second Series, edited by E. S. KENNEDY, M.A. F.R.G.S. With many Maps and Illustrations. 2 vols. square crown 8vo. 42*s.*

Nineteen Maps of the Alpine Districts, from the First and Second Series of *Peaks, Passes, and Glaciers.* Price 7*s.* 6*d.*

The **DOLOMITE MOUNTAINS.** Excursions through Tyrol, Carinthia, Carniola, and Friuli in 1861, 1862, and 1863. By J. GILBERT and G. C. CHURCHILL, F.R.G.S. With numerous Illustrations. Square crown 8vo. 21s.

MOUNTAINEERING in 1861; a Vacation Tour. By Prof. J. TYNDALL, F.R.S. Square crown 8vo. with 2 Views, 7s. 6d.

A **SUMMER TOUR** in the **GRISONS and ITALIAN VALLEYS** of the Bernina. By Mrs. HENRY FRESHFIELD. With 2 Coloured Maps and 4 Views. Post 8vo. 10s. 6d.

Alpine Byeways; or, Light Leaves gathered in 1859 and 1860. By the same Authoress. Post 8vo. with Illustrations, 10s. 6d.

A **LADY'S TOUR ROUND MONTE ROSA**; including Visits to the Italian Valleys. With Map and Illustrations. Post 8vo. 14s.

GUIDE to the **PYRENEES**, for the use of Mountaineers. By CHARLES PACKE. With Maps, &c. and a new Appendix. Fcp. 6s.

GUIDE to the **CENTRAL ALPS**, including the Bernese Oberland, Eastern Switzerland, Lombardy, and Western Tyrol. By JOHN BALL, M.R.I.A. Post 8vo. with 8 Maps, 7s. 6d. or with an INTRODUCTION on Alpine Travelling, and on the Geology of the Alps, 8s. 6d. The INTRODUCTION separately, 1s.

Guide to the Western Alps. By the same Author. With an Article on the Geology of the Alps by M. E. DESOR. Post 8vo. with Maps, &c. 7s. 6d.

A **WEEK** at the **LAND'S END.** By J. T. BLIGHT; assisted by E. H. RODD, R. Q. COUCH, and J. RALFS. With Map and 96 Woodcuts. Fcp. 8vo. 6s. 6d.

VISITS to **REMARKABLE PLACES**: Old Halls, Battle-Fields, and Scenes Illustrative of Striking Passages in English History and Poetry. By WILLIAM HOWITT. 2 vols. square crown 8vo. with Wood Engravings, price 25s.

The **RURAL LIFE of ENGLAND.** By the same Author. With Woodcuts by Bewick and Williams. Medium 8vo. 12s. 6d.

Works of Fiction.

LATE LAURELS: a Tale. By the Author of 'Wheat and Tares.' 2 vols. post 8vo. 15s.

GRYLL GRANGE. By the Author of 'Headlong Hall.' Post 8vo. price 7s. 6d.

A **FIRST FRIENDSHIP.** [Reprinted from *Fraser's Magazine.*] Crown 8vo. 7s. 6d.

THALATTA; or, the Great Commoner: a Political Romance. Crown 8vo. 9s.

ATHERSTONE PRIORY. By L. N. COMYN. 2 vols. post 8vo. 21s.

Ellice : a Tale. By the same. Post 8vo. 9s. 6d.

The LAST of the OLD SQUIRES. By the Rev. J. W. WARTER, B.D. Second Edition. Fcp. 8vo. 4s. 6d.

TALES and STORIES by the Author of 'Amy Herbert,' uniform Edition, each Story or Tale in a single Volume.

AMY HERBERT, 2s. 6d.
GERTRUDE, 2s. 6d.
EARL'S DAUGHTER, 2s. 6d.
EXPERIENCE OF LIFE, 2s. 6d.
CLEVE HALL, 3s. 6d.

IVORS, 3s. 6d.
KATHARINE ASHTON, 3s. 6d.
MARGARET PERCIVAL, 5s.
LANETON PARSONAGE, 4s. 6d.
URSULA, 4s. 6d.

A Glimpse of the World. By the Author of 'Amy Herbert.' Fcp. 7s. 6d.

ESSAYS on FICTION ; comprising Articles on Sir W. SCOTT, Sir E. B. LYTTON, Colonel SENIOR, Mr. THACKERAY, and Mrs. BEECHER STOWE. Reprinted chiefly from the *Edinburgh, Quarterly,* and *Westminster Reviews* ; with large Additions. By NASSAU W. SENIOR. Post 8vo. 10s. 6d.

The GLADIATORS : A Tale of Rome and Judæa. By G. J. WHYTE MELVILLE. Crown 8vo.

Digby Grand, an Autobiography. By the same Author. 1 vol. 5s.

Kate Coventry, an Autobiography. By the same. 1 vol. 5s.

General Bounce, or the Lady and the Locusts. By the same. 1 vol. 5s.

Holmby House, a Tale of Old Northamptonshire. 1 vol. 5s.

Good for Nothing, or All Down Hill. By the same. 1 vol. 6s.

The Queen's Maries, a Romance of Holyrood. 1 vol. 6s.

The Interpreter, a Tale of the War. By the same. 1 vol. 5s.

TALES from GREEK MYTHOLOGY. By the Rev. G. W. COX, M.A. late Scholar of Trin. Coll. Oxon. Second Edition. Square 16mo. 3s. 6d.

Tales of the Gods and Heroes. By the same Author. Second Edition. Fcp. 8vo. 5s.

Tales of Thebes and Argos. By the same Author. Fcp. 8vo. 4s. 6d.

The WARDEN : a Novel. By ANTHONY TROLLOPE. Crown 8vo. 3s. 6d.

Barchester Towers : a Sequel to 'The Warden.' By the same Author. Crown 8vo. 5s.

The SIX SISTERS of the VALLEYS : an Historical Romance. By W. BRAMLEY-MOORE, M.A. Incumbent of Gerrard's Cross, Bucks. With 14 Illustrations on Wood. Crown 8vo. 5s.

Poetry and the Drama.

MOORE'S POETICAL WORKS, Cheapest Editions complete in 1 vol. including the Autobiographical Prefaces and Author's last Notes, which are still copyright. Crown 8vo. ruby type, with Portrait, 7s. 6d. or People's Edition, in larger type, 12s. 6d.

Moore's Poetical Works, as above, Library Edition, medium 8vo. with Portrait and Vignette, 21s. or in 10 vols. fcp. 3s. 6d. each.

TENNIEL'S EDITION of MOORE'S LALLA ROOKH, with 68 Wood Engravings from original Drawings and other Illustrations. Fcp. 4to. 21s.

Moore's Lalla Rookh. 32mo. Plate, 1s. 16mo. Vignette, 2s. 6d. Square crown 8vo. with 13 Plates, 15s.

MACLISE'S EDITION of MOORE'S IRISH MELODIES, with 161 Steel Plates from Original Drawings. Super-royal 8vo. 31s. 6d.

Moore's Irish Melodies, 32mo. Portrait, 1s. 16mo. Vignette, 2s. 6d. Square crown 8vo. with 13 Plates, 21s.

SOUTHEY'S POETICAL WORKS, with the Author's last Corrections and copyright Additions. Library Edition, in 1 vol. medium 8vo. with Portrait and Vignette, 14s. or in 10 vols. fcp. 3s. 6d. each.

LAYS of ANCIENT ROME; with *Ivry* and the *Armada.* By the Right Hon. LORD MACAULAY. 16mo. 4s. 6d.

Lord Macaulay's Lays of Ancient Rome. With 90 Illustrations on Wood, Original and from the Antique, from Drawings by G. SCHARF. Fcp. 4to. 21s.

POEMS. By JEAN INGELOW. Seventh Edition. Fcp. 8vo. 5s.

POETICAL WORKS of LETITIA ELIZABETH LANDON (L. E. L.) 2 vols. 16mo. 10s.

PLAYTIME with the POETS: a Selection of the best English Poetry for the use of Children. By a LADY. Crown 8vo. 5s.

The REVOLUTIONARY EPICK. By the Right Hon. BENJAMIN DISRAELI. Fcp. 8vo. 5s.

BOWDLER'S FAMILY SHAKSPEARE, cheaper Genuine Edition, complete in 1 vol. large type, with 36 Woodcut Illustrations, price 14s. or with the same ILLUSTRATIONS, in 6 pocket vols. 5s. each.

An ENGLISH TRAGEDY; Mary Stuart, from SCHILLER; and Mdlle. De Belle Isle, from A. DUMAS,—each a Play in 5 Acts, by FRANCES ANNE KEMBLE. Post 8vo. 12s.

Rural Sports, &c.

ENCYCLOPÆDIA of RURAL SPORTS; a complete Account, Historical, Practical, and Descriptive, of Hunting, Shooting, Fishing, Racing, &c. By D. P. BLAINE. With above 600 Woodcuts (20 from Designs by JOHN LEECH). 8vo. 42s.

COL. HAWKER'S INSTRUCTIONS to YOUNG SPORTSMEN in all that relates to Guns and Shooting. Revised by the Author's SON. Square crown 8vo. with Illustrations, 18s.

NOTES on RIFLE SHOOTING. By Captain HEATON, Adjutant of the Third Manchester Rifle Volunteer Corps. Fcp. 8vo. 2s. 6d.

The **DEAD SHOT**, or Sportsman's Complete Guide; a Treatise on the Use of the Gun, Dog-breaking, Pigeon-shooting, &c. By MARKSMAN. Fcp. 8vo. with Plates, 5s.

The **CHASE of the WILD RED DEER in DEVON and SOMERSET.** By C. P. COLLYNS. With Map and Illustrations. Square crown 8vo. 16s.

The **FLY-FISHER'S ENTOMOLOGY.** By ALFRED RONALDS. With coloured Representations of the Natural and Artificial Insect. 6th Edition; with 20 coloured Plates. 8vo. 14s.

HANDBOOK of ANGLING : Teaching Fly-fishing, Trolling, Bottom-fishing, Salmon-fishing; with the Natural History of River Fish, and the best modes of Catching them. By EPHEMERA. Fcp. Woodcuts, 5s.

The **CRICKET FIELD** ; or, the History and the Science of the Game of Cricket. By J. PYCROFT, B.A. Trin. Coll. Oxon. 4th Edition. Fcp. 8vo. 5s.

The **Cricket Tutor** ; a Treatise exclusively Practical. By the same. 18mo. 1s.

The **HORSE'S FOOT, and HOW to KEEP IT SOUND.** By W. MILES, Esq. 9th Edition, with Illustrations. Imp. 8vo. 12s. 6d.

A Plain Treatise on Horse-Shoeing. By the same Author. Post 8vo. with Illustrations, 2s.

General Remarks on Stables, and Examples of Stable Fittings. By the same. Imp. 8vo. with 13 Plates, 15s.

Remarks on Horses' Teeth, adapted to Purchasers. By the same Author. Crown 8vo. 1s. 6d.

The **HORSE** : with a Treatise on Draught. By WILLIAM YOUATT. New Edition, revised and enlarged. 8vo. with numerous Woodcuts, 10s. 6d.

The **Dog.** By the same Author. 8vo. with numerous Woodcuts, 6s.

The **DOG in HEALTH and DISEASE.** By STONEHENGE. With 70 Wood Engravings. Square crown 8vo. 15s.

The **Greyhound.** By the same. With many Illustrations. Square crown 8vo. 21s.

The **OX** ; his Diseases and their Treatment: with an Essay on Parturition in the Cow. By J. R. DOBSON, M.R.C.V.S. Post 8vo. with Illustrations. *[Just ready.*

Commerce, Navigation, and Mercantile Affairs.

The LAW of NATIONS Considered as Independent Political Communities. By TRAVERS TWISS, D.C.L. Regius Professor of Civil Law in the University of Oxford. 2 vols. 8vo. 30s. or separately, PART I. *Peace*, 12s. PART II. *War*, 18s.

A DICTIONARY, Practical, Theoretical, and Historical, of Commerce and Commercial Navigation. By J. R. M'CULLOCH, Esq. 8vo. with Maps and Plans, 50s.

The STUDY of STEAM and the **MARINE ENGINE,** for Young Sea Officers. By S. M. SAXBY, R.N. Post 8vo. with 87 Diagrams, 5s. 6d.

A NAUTICAL DICTIONARY, defining the Technical Language relative to the Building and Equipment of Sailing Vessels and Steamers, &c. By ARTHUR YOUNG. Second Edition; with Plates and 150 Woodcuts. 8vo. 18s.

A MANUAL for NAVAL CADETS. By J. M'NEIL BOYD, late Captain R.N. Third Edition; with 240 Woodcuts and 11 coloured Plates. Post 8vo. 12s. 6d.

*** Every Cadet in the Royal Navy is required by the Regulations of the Admiralty to have a copy of this work on his entry into the Navy.

Works of Utility and General Information.

MODERN COOKERY for PRIVATE FAMILIES, reduced to a System of Easy Practice in a Series of carefully-tested Receipts. By ELIZA ACTON. Newly revised and enlarged; with 8 Plates, Figures, and 150 Woodcuts. Fcp. 8vo. 7s. 6d.

On FOOD and its DIGESTION; an Introduction to Dietetics. By W. BRINTON, M.D. Physician to St. Thomas's Hospital, &c. With 48 Woodcuts. Post 8vo. 12s.

ADULTERATIONS DETECTED; or Plain Instructions for the Discovery of Frauds in Food and Medicine. By A. H. HASSALL, M.D. Crown 8vo. with Woodcuts, 17s. 6d.

The VINE and its FRUIT, in relation to the Production of Wine. By JAMES L. DENMAN. Crown 8vo. 8s. 6d.

WINE, the VINE, and the CELLAR. By THOMAS G. SHAW. With 28 Illustrations on Wood. 8vo. 16s.

A PRACTICAL TREATISE on BREWING; with Formulæ for Public Brewers, and Instructions for Private Families. By W. BLACK. 8vo. 10s. 6d.

SHORT WHIST; its Rise, Progress, and Laws; with the Laws of Piquet, Cassino, Ecarté, Cribbage, and Backgammon. By Major A. Fcp. 8vo. 3s.

HINTS on **ETIQUETTE** and the **USAGES of SOCIETY** ; with a Glance at Bad Habits. Revised, with Additions, by a LADY of RANK. Fcp. 8vo. 2s. 6d.

The **CABINET LAWYER** ; a Popular Digest of the Laws of England, Civil and Criminal. 19th Edition, extended by the Author ; including the Acts of the Sessions 1862 and 1863. Fcp. 8vo. 10s. 6d.

The **PHILOSOPHY of HEALTH** ; or, an Exposition of the Physiological and Sanitary Conditions conducive to Human Longevity and Happiness. By SOUTHWOOD SMITH, M.D. Eleventh Edition, revised and enlarged : with New Plates. 8vo. [Just ready.

HINTS to **MOTHERS** on the **MANAGEMENT** of their **HEALTH** during the Period of Pregnancy and in the Lying-in Room. By T. BULL, M.D. Fcp. 8vo. 5s.

The **Maternal Management of Children in Health and Disease.** By the same Author. Fcp. 8vo. 5s.

NOTES on **HOSPITALS.** By FLORENCE NIGHTINGALE. Third Edition, enlarged ; with 13 Plans. Post 4to. 18s.

C. M. WILLICH'S POPULAR TABLES for ascertaining the Value of Lifehold, Leasehold, and Church Property, Renewal Fines, &c.; the Public Funds ; Annual Average Price and Interest on Consols from 1731 to 1861 ; Chemical, Geographical, Astronomical, Trigonometrical Tables, &c. Post 8vo. 10s.

THOMSON'S TABLES of INTEREST, at Three, Four, Four and a Half, and Five per Cent. from One Pound to Ten Thousand and from 1 to 365 Days. 12mo. 3s. 6d.

MAUNDER'S TREASURY of KNOWLEDGE and **LIBRARY** of Reference : comprising an English Dictionary and Grammar, a Universal Gazetteer, a Classical Dictionary, a Chronology, a Law Dictionary, a Synopsis of the Peerage, useful Tables, &c. Fcp. 8vo. 10s.

General and School Atlases.

An **ELEMENTARY ATLAS of HISTORY and GEOGRAPHY,** from the commencement of the Christian Era to the Present Time, in 16 coloured Maps, chronologically arranged, with illustrative Memoirs. By the Rev. J. S. BREWER, M.A. Royal 8vo. 12s. 6d.

SCHOOL ATLAS of PHYSICAL, POLITICAL, and COMMERCIAL GEOGRAPHY, in 17 full-coloured Maps, accompanied by descriptive Letterpress. By E. HUGHES, F.R.A.S. Royal 8vo. 10s. 6d.

BISHOP BUTLER'S ATLAS of ANCIENT GEOGRAPHY, in a Series of 24 full-coloured Maps, accompanied by a complete Accentuated Index New Edition, corrected and enlarged. Royal 8vo. 12s.

BISHOP BUTLER'S ATLAS of MODERN GEOGRAPHY, in a Series of 33 full-coloured Maps, accompanied by a complete Alphabetical Index. New Edition, corrected and enlarged.　Royal 8vo. 10s. 6d.

In consequence of the rapid advance of geographical discovery, and the many recent changes, through political causes, in the boundaries of various countries, it has been found necessary thoroughly to revise this long-established Atlas, and to add several new Maps. New Maps have been given of the following countries: *Palestine*, *Canada*, and the adjacent provinces of *New Brunswick*, *Nova Scotia*, and *Newfoundland*, the *American States* bordering on the Pacific, *Eastern Australia*, and *New Zealand*. In addition to these Maps of *Western Australia* and *Tasmania* have been given in compartments; thus completing the revision of the Map of *Australasia*, rendered necessary by the rising importance of our Australasian possessions. In the Map of *Europe*, *Iceland* has also been re-drawn, and the new boundaries of *France*, *Italy*, and *Austria* represented. The Maps of the three last-named countries have been carefully revised. The Map of *Switzerland* has been wholly re-drawn, showing more accurately the physical features of the country. *Africa* has been carefully compared with the discoveries of LIVINGSTONE, BURTON, SPEKE, BARTH, and other explorers. The number of Maps is thus raised from Thirty to Thirty-three. An entirely new Index has been constructed; and the price of the work has been reduced from 12s. to Half-a-Guinea. The present edition, therefore, will be found much superior to former ones; and the Publishers feel assured that it will maintain the character which this work has so long enjoyed as a popular and comprehensive School Atlas.

MIDDLE-CLASS ATLAS of GENERAL GEOGRAPHY, in a Series of 29 full-coloured Maps, containing the most recent Territorial Changes and Discoveries.　By WALTER M'LEOD, F.R.G.S.　4to. 5s.

PHYSICAL ATLAS of GREAT BRITAIN and IRELAND: comprising 30 full-coloured Maps, with illustrative Letterpress, forming a Concise Synopsis of British Physical Geography.　By WALTER M'LEOD, F.R.G.S. Fcp. 4to. 7s. 6d.

Periodical Publications.

The **EDINBURGH REVIEW**, or **CRITICAL JOURNAL**, published Quarterly in January, April, July, and October.　8vo. price 6s. each No.

The **GEOLOGICAL MAGAZINE**, or Monthly Journal of Geology, edited by T. RUPERT JONES, F.G.S. assisted by HENRY WOODWARD, F.G.S. 8vo. price 1s. 6d. each No.

FRASER'S MAGAZINE for **TOWN** and **COUNTRY**, published on the 1st of each Month.　8vo. price 2s. 6d. each No.

The **ALPINE JOURNAL**: a Record of Mountain Adventure and Scientific Observation.　By Members of the Alpine Club.　Edited by H. B. GEORGE, M.A. Published Quarterly, May 31, Aug. 31, Nov. 30, Feb. 28. 8vo. price 1s. 6d. each No.

INDEX.

SPOTTISWOODE AND CO., PRINTERS, NEW-STREET SQUARE, LONDON

Check Out More Titles From HardPress Classics Series In this collection we are offering thousands of classic and hard to find books. This series spans a vast array of subjects – so you are bound to find something of interest to enjoy reading and learning about.

Subjects:
Architecture
Art
Biography & Autobiography
Body, Mind &Spirit
Children & Young Adult
Dramas
Education
Fiction
History
Language Arts & Disciplines
Law
Literary Collections
Music
Poetry
Psychology
Science
…and many more.

Visit us at www.hardpress.net

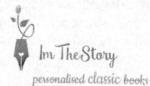

CPSIA information can be obtained
at www.ICGtesting.com
Printed in the USA
BVHW041719220819
556561BV00023B/5763/P